IDEAS & ISSUES
Advanced

Martin Hunt

IDEAS & ISSUES

Advanced

Editor: Diana Bateman
Designer: Valerie Sargent
Cover Design: Gregor Arthur
Photo Researcher: Veena Holkar
Proof-reader: Peter Jenkins

ISBN 3-12-508423-7

Ideas & Issues Listening Cassette: ISBN 3-12-508424-5
Ideas & Issues Listening CD: ISBN 3-12-508435-0

1st edition $^{6\ 5\ 4\ 3}$ 2007   2006   2005   2004

Printed by:
C. Canale & C. S.p.a.
Italy

IDEAS & ISSUES
Advanced

Acknowledgements

The publishers would like to thank the following for their kind permission to use articles and extracts from copyright material:

BBC Online for the articles *TV brings eating disorders to Fiji* (p5), *Talking Point: Are beauty contests outdated?* (p10), the information on IVF (p54) and *Transplants from animals raise the question of spreading disease* (p56); The *Big Issue* for the article *I love my electronic ball and chain* (p12); *Boom!* for the article *Naughty Amsterdam* (p16); Simon Brooke for the article *Homeboys* taken from *Midweek* magazine (p28); Express Syndication for the article *Pedalling is heart to beat* by Philip Douglas (p15); The *Guardian* for the articles *Silent witnesses* by Hugh Brody (p30) *A story nobody told* by Roy Greenslade (p44) and *A lonely planet? Not remotely* by Emily Barr (p52); The *Independent on Sunday* for the article *Trade wars – the hidden tentacles of the world's most secret body'* by Geoffrey Lean (p24); The *Sunday Independent* for the article *No need to apologise for BMWs and blondes* by Mary Ellen Synon (p32); Los Angeles Times Syndicate International for the article *Why don't Asia's heroes look Asian?* by Nuri Vittachi taken from *Time* magazine (p48); The *Mail on Sunday*, The *Daily Mail* and Solo Syndication for the articles *Sport must decide if it really wants to take a moral stand* by Michael Herd as appeared in The *Evening Standard* (p8) and *My Internet hell* by Kate Ginn (p40); *Marie Claire* magazine for the articles *Men forced to be wives* by Denise Dowling (p34) and *What is your wardrobe worth?* (p18); The *Mirror* for the letter *Husband's fallen for his cyberlove* (p41) and the article *Single out the selfish breeders* by Sue Carroll (p50) © Mirror Syndication International 1999; The *New Zealand Herald* for the article *Church doctrine barrier to Pacific fight against AIDS* (p20); The *Observer* for the article *Life Support* by Andrew Smith (p38); The *Philadelphia Daily News* for the article *Experts fear start of 'road rage' trend* by Don Russell (p14); Lawrence Robinson for the article *A slight hitch* taken from *Arena* magazine (p36); The *Telegraph* for the articles *Students make an exhibition of themselves* by Nigel Reynolds (p6), *Girls are turning to violent crime* by Philip Johnston (p58) and *Parents fit secret cameras to spy on their children* (p59) © The Telegraph Group Limited, London, 1998; The *Times* for the articles *A life in the day of Rachel Fentem* (p4), *Dome sculptures show bleak side of British* by Nicholas Hellen (p42), *No sex, no violence, just film* by Geoff Brown (p60) © Times Newspapers Limited, 1999; The Toronto Star Syndicate for the articles *Food labelling too much to swallow* by Michael Landsberg (p22) and *Today's leaders live in a cocoon of privilege* by Carol Goar (p26); The *Washington Post* for the article *American pop penetrates worldwide* by Paul Farhi and Megan Rosenfeld (p2); Barry Wigmore for the article *Black and white test-tube twins shock for mum* taken from The *Sun* (p54).

Photographs

The publishers would like to thank the following for their kind permission to reproduce photographs, illustrations and cartoons:

The Bridgeman Art Library for the photograph of *Three Flags* by Jasper Johns (p3); Bubbles for the photograph of the girl weighing herself (p4), the smartly dressed woman (p18) and the family (p28) © Bubbles; Cartoonstock for the cartoons (pages 2, 7, 9, 19, 22, 33, 35, 37, 39, 41, 44, 46, 49, 53, 59 and 61); Jan Chipps Photography for the photograph of the casually dressed woman (p18), the photograph of the bottle of champagne (p32) and the photograph of the Millennium Dome (p42); Colorific! for the photograph of tobacco pickers (p24); The *Daily Mail* for the photograph of Emma Gibson (p40); Empics Ltd for the photograph of the runner on the cover and Ben Johnson (p8) © Empics Ltd; Environment images for the photograph of the doctor on the cover; The *Guardian* for the photograph by David Sillitoe of *Mother and Child Divided* by Damien Hirst © The *Guardian*; Impact for the photograph of the teenage boy smoking marijuana (p16) and the Iranian schoolgirl (p60); Life File for the photograph of two Greek women (p34); Hayley Maddon for the photograph of the tagged ankle (p12); Dr Yorgos Nikas/The Science Photo Library for the photograph of the 16-cell embryo (p54); The Picture Library, National Portrait Gallery, London, for the Gerald Scarfe cartoon of Margaret Thatcher (p43); PA News Photo Library for the photograph of Benjamin Netanyahu and his family (p27) and of the transgenic pigs (p56); Popperfoto for the photograph of prisoners in Leeds Prison (p13) © Popperfoto/Reuters; The Telegraph Colour Library for the photograph of Europe from space the female figure in cyberspace on the cover and the photograph of harvesting wheat (p25), the Sahara bushman (p30), the wedding cake decorations (p36) the Moon (p38) and the mother and child (p51); Frank Spooner Pictures for the photograph of Miss World 1998 (p11), the AIDS patient (p21) and the photograph from the film *Superman* (p48) © Gamma; Tony Stone Images for the photograph of the cyclist (p15) the fortune teller (p47), the group of backpackers (p52) and the group of girls (p58) © Tony Stone Images.

Every effort has been made to contact the copyright holders of material used in this book. The publishers apologise for any omissions and will be pleased to make the necessary arrangements when the title is reprinted.

Contents

Using *Ideas and Issues Advanced*

What is special about *Ideas and Issues Advanced*?

- It offers a broad range of interesting, provocative and relevant topics that increase students' awareness of global issues

- It contains challenging authentic texts as a springboard for debate

- The texts balance personal opinions with well-researched facts

- It gives students the opportunity to debate relevant issues through guided discussion questions

- It allows students to personalise and share information about themselves, their country, and their culture

- There are challenging writing tasks as a follow up

- It provides an information resource for students, as well as a guide to further research

- It is creating, stimulating and fun – for both students and teachers

Objectives of *Ideas and Issues Advanced*

The aim of *Ideas and Issues* is to encourage learners to explore different issues through a variety of sources and to transfer their reading skills to speaking skills. Students are encouraged to process information from different sources to back up their opinions in a discussion or debate. To facilitate this, there are phrases presented on easy-to-use flaps that enable students to present their opinions and back up their ideas. By using stimulating articles on a variety of topics that students might read in their own language, the book encourages self-expression. Students are encouraged to explore the moral dimensions behind fundamental global issues. The book enables students to explore other cultures, not just those of the UK and Europe and cross-cultural comparison is encouraged.

Selection of articles

Each article has been specifically chosen to arouse students' interests and provoke lively debate. The subject matter ranges from the serious, such as *News blackout* and *Global control*, to the more light-hearted *Fashion statement* and *Home, sweet home*. Each topic can be approached from different angles, with ample opportunity to explore the moral and philosophical dimensions of each topic. Some issues are controversial and it is up to the teacher to decide what material can be covered in class. The articles are suitable for upper-intermediate to advanced students.

Articles

All the reading texts are authentic. A variety of sources has been used – including newspapers, magazines and websites, so that students can experience a variety of styles, not just broadsheet newspapers, but also tabloid and magazine articles. While the majority of articles have come from the UK, articles are also included from other English speaking countries, including pieces from the US, Canada and New Zealand. All the articles have been chosen for their youth appeal and because the topics covered will remain relevant for years to come. Some issues are controversial as befits a book on modern-day issues. So issues such as drug control, AIDS and racism are explored. Care has been taken to balance the journalists' point of view with factual information on the issue so that a balanced argument is presented. Also, any intrusive discussion questions have been avoided. However, it is up to the teacher to decide what questions might be unsuitable for the class and these can be ignored. All units relate to broader issues, so that if one line of discussion fails, another can be explored. Units such as *Global control* focus on political issues, while others such as *Home, sweet home* and *Marriage* focus on issues from a more personal angle.

Class planning and management

Each unit is two pages long. No unit needs to be covered in its entirety in any one class. If the issue is especially complex, then it could be covered over two or even three classes. For example, the role-play could be left until the next session and the *Networking* section could be used for project work. As a rough guide each unit could take up to one and a half to two hours.

As *Ideas and Issues Advanced* has been written as a supplementary resource book, preparation can be minimal, but in order to get the most out of each unit, teachers could consider the following points before each class.

- Check what sort of a linguistic challenge the article is going to pose for students.

- Look at the comprehension questions to familiarise yourself with the answers. Think about the students' knowledge of the subject area – do they need extra help?

- Will you set research tasks before the lesson so students can bring more factual knowledge to the discussion questions? Or will the students do this in follow-up lessons?

- Think of points to make yourself in order to warm the class up if they are slow to provide ideas – and also set any supplementary questions that might be appropriate.

- Are there any discussion questions you might want to miss out on grounds of sensitivity?

- Finally, think about what you expect from the class. How will they cope linguistically? Are there any structures (such as language of agreement or disagreement) that need covering before using this book? (The language presented in the speaking strategies pull out is intended as an aid rather than a presentation.) How will students cope with the ideas involved? How can the class dynamics be manipulated to produce the best results?

Student preparation

In order to maximise class speaking time, students could read the article as homework and check any new vocabulary in the word list. For certain topics, students could even do some research and look at the websites suggested in the *Networking* section.

Topic sources

The articles come from a variety of sources. The views expressed in the articles are those of the journalists and are not necessarily endorsed by the publishers.

A guide to getting round the Internet

The Internet can be an invaluable resource for finding out more about certain issues. It is also a good source for finding foreign newspapers. The information below is intended to help students and teachers get the best from the web and use it as an extra resource.

- **Web pages and URL** (*Universal Resource Locator*) **boxes**

Web pages can look daunting, but once you have understood the basics, they are easy to use. When you start an Internet browser program (one that's designed to let you see what's on the Internet – often Internet Explorer or Netscape Navigator), two windows of information appear. The large window (usually full of text and pictures) is the **web page** itself. The smaller window is the **location** you're at (often called the **URL**). The first thing to note is that, when it comes to the URL, you must type in the correct location

(or address) or the Internet will be unable to find the site. And if you write it down for later reference, check you have written the address correctly.

The **web page** contains the information you want. A web site is, quite simply, a collection of web pages. The first page in a site serves as an index or entry, and is known as the **home page**. To get to the other pages follow the links. These are easy to find and are generally written in blue and underlined. Alternatively, there might be a picture or an icon to follow. An easy way to see if it's a link is to place the mouse cursor over it. If the arrow turns into a little hand, it means it's a link.

- **Search Engines and bookmarks**

Imagine the Internet is a huge colour encyclopaedia. You might want to research a certain subject. You could guess an address and type it in the URL window, but **search engines** are very useful for this.

Search engines will do the work for you. They will search through the Internet and give you a list of 'hits' – that is, pages that have information on the subject you are searching for. There is a lot of information available. You may need to refine your search. A search for James Bond, for example, will look for information on *James* and *Bond* – and may list sites you're not interested in. One thing you can do is to use an **advanced search**. By typing *and* you specify both words must appear, by typing *or* you show either is acceptable. Some search engines use " " marks to show an entry is a proper name. If you want to try a search engine, try Yahoo! (www.yahoo.com) as a starter. Type your search in the box and follow the link to the advanced search options to help you optimise your search (don't forget there are many other search engines available – Yahoo! lists many of them itself).

Once you have found a page on the Internet that is useful you can **bookmark** it. Click on **Bookmarks** in the menu, and you will see a command to add a bookmark, as well as a list of bookmarks already saved. Clicking on Bookmarks will take you instantly to the page you require.

There is only so much advice to give. The best tip is to familiarise yourself with the Internet. It will quickly become far easier to use than you might think and if used wisely, can be an invaluable resource.

Some starter links:

www.amazon.com	A big online bookseller with many local subsidiaries (e.g. in the UK, www.amazon.co.uk)
www.britannica.com	An online encyclopaedia
www.esicafe.com	Dave Sperling's ESL cafe; a great place to start for EFL/ESL resources on the web
www.infoplease.com	An online encyclopaedia
www.thepaperboy.com	An excellent set of links to international newspapers
www.us.imdb.com	The Internet movie database
www.yahoo.com	One of the most popular search engines on the web

Speaking strategies

These play an essential part of an effective discussion. The strategies are presented on specific functional headings on pull-out flaps. Basic speaking strategies are presented on the front flaps while more complex ones appear on the back flap.

How to choose a unit

As this is a supplementary book rather than a coursebook, there is no linear progression of difficulty. The units are presented alphabetically, so it is up to the teacher to choose the appropriate topic. Some units could work well together, for example *Male crisis* and *Violent youth, American supremacy* and *Lost language, Anorexia* and *Beauty*. Treat the book as a resource, selecting issues to suit the interests of the class, or ones that are currently in the news. Each unit stands alone and should be chosen according to its length and suitability.

Structure of units

Each unit follows the same pattern:

- Focus
- Reading
- Comprehension
- Ammunition Box
- Discussion
- Activities
- Networking

Contents of the unit

All the units follow a standard layout of two pages. Each unit allows maximum flexibility, depending on the level and size of the class and the time available. The *Focus* section should be covered first, followed by the article. After that, it is up to the teacher to decide which elements to work on. The *Ammunition Box* can be used alongside the *Discussion* and *Activities* section.

🎯 FOCUS

Focus is the pre-reading activity designed to lead the students into the subject matter of the article. It allows the students to express their ideas and opinions on the subject before exploring it in more depth.

Reading

Each unit contains one, sometimes, two articles that act as a springboard for discussion. Students could be encouraged to pre-read longer articles at home, but in general these can be read aloud or listened to in class.

??? COMPREHENSION

This section covers basic comprehension of the article, but also tests the students' ability to understand inferences, as well as reading between the lines, both important skills at this level. It is vital to get students to justify their answers, ideally using functional language (*I think/ because*). As the texts are authentic, the vocabulary can be challenging so students should be encouraged to use the word list at the back of the book.

"Good evening, we'd like to talk to you about genetically modified crops"

🎩 DISCUSSION

The *Discussion* section includes indirect comprehension questions, but also aims to stimulate new areas of debate. This then broadens into wider reflections on the topic as a whole. There has been a conscious effort not only to encourage students to express their own opinions (and again, it's vital to get the students to explain *why* they hold these views) but also to share their personal experiences and discuss what happens in their own countries/culture. Again, sensitivity is required – the questions have been designed not to be intrusive, but it is up to the teacher to judge which questions are appropriate.

🕐 AMMUNITION BOX

The *Ammunition Box* is designed primarily as an aid to the discussion questions. It includes useful vocabulary on the topic area (**Key words**) and extra factual information (**Handy hints**) so that the students can put the issue into a wider context. Encourage students to refer to it in their discussion.

🏃 ACTIVITIES

There are two types of activities: speaking and writing. The Speaking activity involves pair work, group work and role-play. These activities practise group dynamics, and the use of appropriate structures (*I think / Do you agree? / What about? / This would be a better idea because*) should be encouraged. The problem solving situations involving inter-student communication are becoming more common in exams, so this section could be useful for students studying for exams. The role play activities are best suited to groups of four or five. Although the situation will have been roughly outlined, it is important that the students use their imagination and invent extra details. This can then be followed by class feedback where the students can compare their results with each other.

The Writing activity usually involves a follow up to the speaking section or the article. This includes writing letters, reports or newspaper articles. There are also essay questions. Students are encouraged to borrow ideas from other. Some thought has been given to exams here, as students are asked to stick to a particular subject and task, as well as provide a variety of formats (letters, reports, and essays).

🌐 NETWORKING

The *Networking* section gives students the opportunity to work independently and find more information on the subject under discussion. It provides a list of possible sources, such as books, films or Internet sites. This can involve project work, or can be set as homework. The list is not exhaustive, but acts as a starting point for more research. It is important to be aware that there is a lot of information on the web, and it isn't always easy to sift through. Secondly, students might well be distracted by other material, so try to keep your students on track. Encourage them to think of any other material that might be relevant so that the topic under discussion can be broadened to include material from their own country.

WORD LIST

In order to maintain the authenticity of the articles, vocabulary within the text is not highlighted or numbered. Instead, an extensive word list appears at the end of the book on page 62. It includes the definition and the phonetic transcription of each word, and the page on which it appears.

"SORRY I'M LATE. I HAD TO GET A TATTOO REMOVED."

VISUALS

Many units contain visuals which represent an extra resource. Most units contain cartoons which relate to the article and the discussion questions.

The Internet has been useful in providing the author with international papers quickly – one site worth recommending is www.thepaperboy.com This gives a listing of hundreds of online papers, sorted by country, as well as a 'top drawer' listing of recommended papers.

The UK media

Britain comes third after the Japanese and Swedes with a large daily readership. The press is not state-controlled nor linked financially to any political party or union. However, the majority of papers are right-wing and are outspoken in their support of the Conservative party.

The newspapers in the UK are dominated by the national papers rather than regional papers. These papers cover national and international stories. The main regional papers are The *Herald* and The *Scotsman* for Scotland and The *Western Mail* for Wales. Britain also has a tradition of reading Sunday newspapers rather than weekly magazines for an overview of current issues. There is a local press in the UK, but it is less widely read. News magazines are less popular, although *Time* and *Newsweek* (both American) are available.

There are two sorts of newspaper in Britain, broadsheet and tabloid (the paper size of these papers is half that of the broadsheets). There is also a perceived difference in quality between the two. The tabloids are typically more popular. They focus on scandal, gossip and sensation, their articles are shorter and there is less in-depth analysis of issues. The broadsheets are more serious in tone and cover issues in much greater detail. They have increased in size, often

ARENA

Format	Men's magazine
Circulation	46,777
Publication	Monthly
Owner	EMAP
Other	*Arena* is a glossy magazine for men. It contains fashion and articles on contemporary issues. It is aimed at sophisticated, professional men in their thirties.

BBC News Online

Format	BBC news website
Website	www.bbc.co.uk
Other	The BBC online service provides a rich source of information. It includes comment and analysis of the lastest news, plus links to the BBC World Service, News and Education.

BOOM!
From the Boom Chicago Comedy Show

Format	A4 black and white magazine
Circulation	300,000
Publication	Published quarterly
Owner	Boom Chicago
Other	A guide to Amsterdam produced by a group of Americans who moved to Amsterdam and set up a comedy show.

THE BIG ISSUE

Format	A3 weekly newspaper
Circulation	million
Publication	Weekly
Politics	Left of centre
Owner	The Big Issue Ltd
Website	www.bigissue.com
Other	Set up in 1991 to combat homelessness. It is sold by the homeless, and campaigns on their behalf .

Daily Mail

Format	Tabloid British newspaper, in colour
Circulation	2.3 million
Publication	Daily
Politics	Right of centre
Owner	Northcliffe Newspapers
Website	www.dailymail.co.uk
Other	First published in 1896, it also publishes The *Mail on Sunday*. It has a strong financial section, and a high-income, mainly female readership.

The Daily Telegraph

Format	Broadsheet British newspaper, in colour
Circulation	1,042,382
Publication	Daily
Politics	Right of centre
Owner	Hollinger International Inc.
Website	www.dailytelegraph.co.uk
Other	First published in 1855, it is Britain's largest-selling quality daily newspaper and is noted for its finance pages and online edition.

Evening Standard

Format	Tabloid London evening newspaper, in colour
Circulation	453,618
Publication	Daily from midday onwards in London area
Politics	Right of centre
Owner	Associated Newspapers Ltd
Website	www.thisislondon.co.uk
Other	First published in 1827 as The *London Standard*, the paper was bought by Associated Newspapers in 1988. It is the newspaper typically read by London commuters on their way home.

THE EXPRESS

Format	Tabloid British newspaper, in colour
Circulation	1,092,247
Publication	Daily
Politics	Right of centre
Owner	United News and Media
Website	www.express.co.uk

The Guardian

Format	Two-section, broadsheet and tabloid British newspaper with international editions, in colour
Circulation	391,919
Publication	Daily
Politics	Left of centre
Owner	The Scott Trust (for The Guardian Group)
Website	www.theguardian.co.uk
Other	First published in 1821 as The *Manchester Guardian*. It is the second best-selling daily broadsheet newspaper in Britain. It has formal links with leading European newspapers. It also publishes The *Guardian Weekly* (joint association between The *Guardian*, *Le Monde* and The *Washington Post*).

THE INDEPENDENT

Format	Broadsheet British newspaper, in colour
Circulation	222,200
Publication	Daily
Politics	Independent/centre
Owner	Independent Newspapers (UK)
Website	www.independent.co.uk
Other	Launched in 1986 and founded by journalists wanting to be independent from the large media companies. It is noted for its photography and focuses on issues not personalities.

THE INDEPENDENT ON SUNDAY

Format	Broadsheet multiple-section British Sunday newspaper, in colour
Circulation	239,181
Publication	Weekly, every Sunday
Politics	Centre
Owner	Independent Newspapers (UK)
Website	See The *Independent*
Other	See The *Independent*

coming with a second, supplementary section which is tabloid in size and often devoted to a particular subject area (the arts, business, IT). Competition is fierce in the UK market, and few subjects are considered off-limits, especially to the tabloids. The debate on press freedom – for example, in covering the royal family and any photographs used – is in full flow and still unresolved.

Both the British and American press are independent but are often owned by large media corporations, such as Rupert Murdoch's News International in Britain. In America, as in Britain, there is a distinction between tabloid (*USA Today*) and broadsheet (The *New York Times*), and major American quality papers tend to be left of centre. The *New York Times* is highly-respected and the most distributed, but The *Washington Post* is the one that best records

Government decisions. The *Los Angeles Times* and The *Miami Herald* are two other important regional papers, but every city of any size has its own newspaper.

There is a lively magazine market in the UK. There are hundreds of magazines devoted to individual interests (Computing, Gardening, Sport) as well as more general magazines. Women's magazines (*Cosmopolitan, Marie Claire, New Woman*) have been popular for many years, containing a mix of fashion and beauty items along with reports on news stories and issues that affect women. A relatively recent phenomenon has been the rise of the man's magazine (*FHM, Loaded, GQ*) These are less serious in tone than their female counterparts, normally containing a mix of the outrageous and the bizarre.

Sunday Independent

Format	Broadsheet multiple-section Irish Sunday newspaper
Circulation	2,870,000
Publication	Weekly, every Sunday
Politics	Centre
Owner	Independent Newspapers (UK)
Website	www.independent.ie
Other	The Sunday Independent is the best-selling Sunday paper in Ireland.

marie claire

Format	Woman's magazine
Circulation	(incl. export) 437,642
Publication	Monthly
Owner	European Magazines Ltd.

Midweek

Format	Colour magazine for London commuters
Circulation	75,000
Publication	Weekly
Owner	Independent Magazines UK Ltd.
Other	It is London's best read commuter magazine and is distributed free to commuters three times a week outside major underground stations.

The Mirror

Format	Tabloid British newspaper, in colour
Circulation	2,352,576
Publication	Daily
Politics	Left of centre
Owner	Mirror Group
Website	www.mirror.co.uk
Other	Established in 1903.

The Observer

Format	Broadsheet multiple-section British Sunday newspaper, in colour
Circulation	381,101
Publication	Weekly, every Sunday
Politics	Left of centre
Owner	The Scott Trust (for The Guardian Group)
Website	See The *Guardian*
Other	Founded in 1791 it is the oldest Sunday newspaper in the world. It was bought by The *Guardian* in 1993.

PHILADELPHIA DAILY NEWS

Format	Broadsheet American newspaper in colour
Circulation	166,353
Publication	Daily
Politics	Centre
Owner	Philadelphia newspaper Inc.
Website	www.phillynews.com/daily_news

The Sun

Format	Tabloid British newspaper
Circulation	3,685,645
Publication	Daily
Politics	Right of centre
Owner	News International (Rupert Murdoch)
Website	www.currantbun.com
Other	The best-selling daily newspaper in Britain, known for its photos of topless women and provocative headlines. It started in 1912 as The *Daily Herald*.

THE SUNDAY TIMES

Format	Broadsheet multiple-section British Sunday newspaper, in colour
Circulation	1,293,489
Publication	Weekly, every Sunday
Politics	Right of centre
Owner	News International
Website	See *The Times*
Other	Dominates the Sunday quality newspaper market. It has eight sections. Its aim is to cater to everyone. It often focuses on famous personalities.

THE TIMES

Format	Broadsheet British newspaper, in colour
Circulation	709,546
Publication	Daily
Politics	Right of centre
Owner	News International
Website	www.the-times.co.uk
Other	First published in 1875, it is the oldest and most famous British newspaper. It is famous for its letters page and its crosswords. It is the newspaper of the 'establishment' and has a large readership in the south-east of Britain.

TIME

Format	News magazine
Circulation	4,083,387
Publication	Weekly
Politics	Right of centre
Owner	Time Warner Inc.
Website	www.pathfinder.com/time/
Other	Time Magazine was founded 76 years ago and is the largest and most successful news magazine. There are different editions for different regions, including Time Asia, Canada and Europe. Time Warner Inc. also owns Warner Bros and the news channel CNN.

THE TORONTO STAR

Format	Broadsheet Canadian newspaper, in colour
Circulation	450,000
Publication	Published daily in two editions
Politics	Centre
Owner	Torstar Corporation
Website	www.thestar.com
Other	It is Canada's largest daily newspaper.

The Washington Post

Format	Broadsheet American newspaper, in colour
Circulation	783,000
Publication	Daily
Politics	Right of centre
Owner	The Washington Post Company
Website	www.washingtonpost.com
Other	Founded in 1877. It owns *Newsweek* magazine.

THE NEW ZEALAND HERALD

Format	Broadsheet New Zealand newspaper, in colour
Circulation	551,000
Publication	Daily
Politics	Centre
Owner	Independent Newspapers PLC
Website	www.nzherald.co.nz
Other	New Zealand's largest daily newspaper, founded in 1863.

- Think of five films, five TV programmes and five pop songs.
- How many of these were American?

American Pop Penetrates Worldwide

By Paul Farhi and Megan Rosenfeld

America's biggest export is no longer the fruit of its fields or the output of its factories, but the mass-produced products of its popular culture – movies, TV programs, music, books and computer software.

Entertainment around the world is dominated by American-made products. It's 'The Young and the Restless' in New Delhi, Garth Brooks blaring from a Dublin apartment, or the eager line of people waiting outside a Nairobi movie theater to see *As Good as it Gets*. It's Bart Simpson in Seoul, Madonna in São Paulo, Dr Quinn Medicine Woman on Warsaw TV.

Sociologist Todd Gitlin calls American popular culture 'the latest in a long succession of bidders for global unification. It succeeds the Latin imposed by the Roman Empire and the Catholic Church, and Marxist Leninism imposed by Communist governments.

Tom Freston, president of MTV, the globe-straddling music network, sees it another way. 'Today's young people have passports to two different worlds – to their own culture and to ours,' he said.

Once, back when *I Love Lucy* was still in its first run, U.S. made entertainment could be found only in places with the means to buy it, the technology to show it, and the political freedom to allow it across the border. Now, even in tiny Bhutan, a Himalayan nation so isolated that fewer than 5,000 people visit it a year, street peddlers offer illegally copied videos of Hollywood's latest blockbusters.

"I believe you're big in America"

Global consumerism and expanding channels of distribution may create more demand for entertainment, but neither says much about why people prefer the American variety to that produced in, say, Venezuela or Japan or France.

The answer is partly linguistic, partly economic, and partly a reflection of the unique historical, racial and ideological development of the United States. To its admirers, U.S. entertainment is something bright and new. 'The United States has little history and it is very open to new things,' said David Escobar Galindo, El Salvador's foremost writer. 'Europe has many wonderful things, but it is very tied to its past. U.S. culture is fresher.'

Jack Lang, France's former minister of culture who is renowned for his protectionist views, appreciates American culture as 'pure entertainment. It's without restraint, without shame. ... It finds the soul of the child in the adult. This is not pejorative.'

There has long been another view, of course. To religious conservatives, American culture is still the noisy electronic spawn of the Great Satan, undermining traditional values and encouraging wickedness. U.S. movies and television promote mindless consumerism, others complain, and emit a toxic vapor that chokes the wellspring of native creativity.

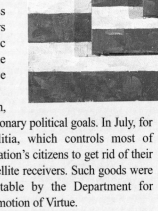

In its most extreme form, this distaste can serve reactionary political goals. In July, for instance, the Taliban militia, which controls most of Afghanistan, ordered that nation's citizens to get rid of their TVs, video players and satellite receivers. Such goods were deemed morally unacceptable by the Department for Prevention of Vice and Promotion of Virtue.

A fair number of Americans might even agree with Fidel Castro's recent critique of the United States' 'canned culture', which he contended 'transmits poisonous messages, in the social and moral order, to all families, to all homes, to all children'.

The Washington Post

1 What is America's biggest export?
2 What was needed in the 1950s to view American culture?
3 How does David Escobar Galindo think the US differs from Europe?
4 In your own words, explain what is meant by 'mindless consumerism'.
5 Explain what Fidel Castro means by 'transmits poisonous messages, in the social and moral order, to all families, to all homes, to all children'.

 DISCUSSION

1 Why do you think American culture has been so successful?

2 How popular is American culture in your country? Do you think this is a good or a bad thing?

3 How else did the United States dominate the 20th century, for instance in politics, business or technology? Give examples.

4 Why/how do you think America managed to dominate the last century?

5 Do you see America as a force for good or bad in the world? Why?

6 What can other countries learn from America? What can America learn from your country?

7 Do you think America will also dominate the next century? Justify your answer? If not, which country/area of the world do you think will take prominence?

8 What other countries are becoming increasingly powerful?

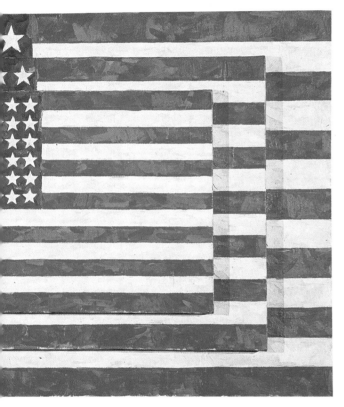

Three Flags, *1958, Jasper Johns*

NETWORKING

How does American culture influence your country? Does your country gain or lose economically, politically and culturally from this influence?

Books: *American Culture: The End of the American Century* by Steven Schlosstein
The American Century: Consensus and Coercion in the Projection of American Power by David Slater, Peter Taylor and Peter J. Taylor
The Lost Continent: Travels in Small Town America by Bill Bryson

Websites:
lcweb.loc.gov/homepage/exhibits.html
sln.fi.edu/tfi/hotlists/government.html
www.unc.edu/sycamore

 ACTIVITIES

A **Work together in groups of four or five. Look back at the 20th century and decide ...**

Who was the greatest sportsman/sportswoman?	The greatest artist?
The greatest musician(s)?	The greatest writer?
The greatest politician?	What was the greatest song?
	The greatest invention?

Be prepared to justify your answer!

Try to come to a joint decision on one name. How many on your list are American? Now compare your list with that of another group – are they similar, or very different?

B ✍ **Write an essay: America has been nothing but a force for evil.**

AMMUNITION BOX

Key words
supremacy *a position of authority*
domination *having control/influence over someone or something*
to impose *to force your beliefs/opinions on someone*
consumerism *the belief that a society or individual needs many goods and services*
culture *art, literature, music and other creative expressions*

Handy hints
- Three quarters of all movies (outside India and Pakistan) are made in Hollywood
- The USA accounts for 25% of world output
- It is the world's richest economy with a gross domestic product (GDP) of approximately $5,500 billion (Bangladesh has a GDP of nearly $25 billion, Indonesia $110 billion, Japan nearly $3,500 billion)
- 57% own a car (as opposed to 37% in Germany, for example)
- There are 1,700 national newspapers (China has 1,775)
- Cable TV is available in 60% of homes (70% in Switzerland)
- The US spends $277.2 billion on its armed forces (Russia spends almost $30 billion, China nearly $7 billion, and the UK just over $40 billion)

- Can someone be 'too thin'? What are some of the medical dangers associated with lack of food?
- What do you know about the medical condition anorexia nervosa? Do you know how it is treated?

RACHEL FENTEM'S DAY

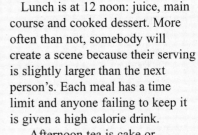

Rachel Fentem, 20, is an inpatient at the Gerald Russell Eating Disorder Unit. Admitted six months ago weighing 4st 12lb (about 32 kilos), she currently weighs 6st (41 kilos).

The call to be weighed comes at 6.30am but I am already awake. I stand on the scales backwards, so I am not thrown into a panic by my increasing weight. In many ways, I am sick of this beast, continually whispering in my ear that I am too fat. Yet I am scared to lose what has become my best friend.

At 8am I stand outside the dining room. I don't want to eat but if I run away, 17 other patients will be sent to find me, forbidden to continue their meal until I return. Breakfast is a big meal: juice, cereal, cooked course and toast. By 8.45 I have already consumed several times the daily calorie ration I would allow myself. Afterwards I have to rest for an hour with the other girls. They are all so fragile and delicate, I feel obese. However low my weight drops, it is never low enough. This is another trick the anorexia plays: by reaching a magical number – a few pounds lighter – I will like and accept myself.

My stomach is uncomfortably bloated from breakfast. This is my fourth hospital admission and each time I have reached a lower weight and found re-feeding more of a struggle.

Some mornings there is a community group. Discussions range from the angrily animated to the sullenly silent. Snacks follow much too soon, at 10am. Then I usually go to an occupational therapy group: art, drama or dance. Time is controlled and I savour my 20-minute pass. I have to resist the urge to run.

Lunch is at 12 noon: juice, main course and cooked dessert. More often than not, somebody will create a scene because their serving is slightly larger than the next person's. Each meal has a time limit and anyone failing to keep it is given a high calorie drink.

Afternoon tea is cake or dreaded chocolate. All foods are difficult but chocolate and puddings are particularly hard. Consumption becomes indulgence and I feel an urge to punish myself with self-induced vomiting.

I fill the afternoon with occupational therapy. By building a trusting relationship with the nurse, I have become more confident that I will not make myself vulnerable if I speak to her.

Dinner is another perennial battleground. It is not uncommon for plates and food to be thrown. By making food and weight loss central to my life, my unhappiness about issues at home and school did not hurt so much. For me, anorexia began with a diet and a comment being made about my weight at a ballet lesson.

The final meal is at 10pm. Most of us are relieved that it is the last. Official bedtime is 12.30 but most have retired before then, mentally and physically washed out.

Sleep does not always come easily, since insomnia is a side effect of being at a low weight.

The Sunday Times

1 What time is Rachel weighed?
2 Why does Rachel stand on the scales backwards?
3 How many times has Rachel been in hospital?
4 What food is particularly difficult for Rachel to eat?
5 What is one of the side effects of anorexia?

'TV brings eating disorders to Fiji'

Fiji, a nation that has traditionally cherished the fuller figure, has been struck by an outbreak of eating disorders since the arrival of television in 1995, according to a recent study. Researchers from Harvard say the western images and values have led to an increase in disorders such as anorexia and bulimia.

In 1998 – 38 months after the station went on air – a survey revealed that 74% of teenage girls felt they were 'too big or fat'. 15% of the girls reported they had vomited to control their weight.

Anne Becker, an anthropologist from Harvard, said: 'Nobody was dieting in Fiji 10 years ago, the teenagers see TV as a model for how one gets by in the modern world.'

Many groups say the worldwide increase in eating disorders is down to the prevalence of images equating a slim figure with beauty.

But some doctors have questioned whether such disorders are caused by culture or are transmitted from generation to generation in genes.

BBC News Online

 DISCUSSION

1 What do you think causes anorexia?

2 Do you think anorexia is a physical or mental illness, or both?

3 Why do you think young people, especially women, feel such pressure to be thin?

4 Should parents and teachers bear some of the responsibility for this pressure? Why, why not?

5 How do you think eating disorders such as anorexia should be treated? Should they involve the patient being treated against his or her will?

6 Do you think an enforced eating regime helps the sufferers, or would therapy get to the heart of the problem?

7 Do you think it is possible for someone with anorexia to be completely cured? If not, why not?

8 Do you think men are becoming more interested in the way they look – and therefore more prone to suffer from eating disorders?

COMPREHENSION

1 When did television arrive in Fiji?
2 What was the traditional Fijian attitude to women's figures?
3 Why are so many teenagers dieting?
4 Why are eating disorders increasing?
5 What other causes of eating disorders are there?

ACTIVITIES

A Debate the following issue: Images in the media are solely to blame for the growth in anorexia among teenagers.

B Imagine you are the parent of an anorexic boy or girl. You can see how ill your child is becoming, despite the fact that the youngster refuses to acknowledge a problem. Who can you ask for advice on how to deal with the situation before it is too late – your partner, the family doctor, a counsellor? Describe your feelings and exactly how you plan to resolve the problem.

 NETWORKING

Find out more about treatments for anorexia and bulimia nervosa in your country. Are these treatments successful?

Books: *Anorexia and Bulimia: Your Questions Answered* (Element Guide Series) by Julia Buckroyd
Diana: Her True Story by Andrew Morton
The Long Road Back, A Survivor's Guide to Anorexia by Judy Tam Sargent

Websites:
www.bbc.co.uk
www.rcpsych.ac.uk

  **AMMUNITION BOX**

Key words
anorexia nervosa *a form of intentional starvation. What begins as a normal diet is taken to extremes*
• Anorexia usually starts in the mid teens. The average age for onset is 16
• It usually affects women from middle-class families
bulimia nervosa *illness involving a cycle of starving and bingeing*
• Bulimia usually affects a slightly older age group – between early and mid-twenties
• It affects three out of 100 women

Handy hints
• Around 5% of young girls in Britain have anorexia
• Around 90% of cases involve females
• Over 25% of anorexics require hospitalisation
• Between 60,000 and 200,000 people in Britain are thought to have anorexia or bulimia – a tenth of them are men
• Only around 60% of anorexics recover
• One in 10 people suffering from anorexia die from the effects of starvation
• 6% of women who develop anorexia or bulimia do so in their thirties: on average they suffer longer – 10 years compared with six years in younger women
• Forms of therapy include group therapy, family counselling, psychotherapy and anti-depressants
• Psychiatrists have singled out several characteristics which they say are typical of anorexics. These include a dominant, over-protective mother and a passive father, a tendency to perfectionism and a strong desire for order

 **FOCUS**

'This is not a good work of art. It seems to me to be on the edge of being a hoax and quite a good joke. I think the joke wins.'

Richard Dorment, art critic of *The Telegraph*

Students make an exhibition of themselves

By Nigel Reynolds, Arts Correspondent

THIRTEEN art students given a grant and sponsorship of £1,600 to put on an exhibition spent the money on a week's holiday on the Costa del Sol and returned home claiming that the trip was conceptual art.

Two sponsors, including the Leeds University students' union, which gave a grant of £1,126, said they had been misled by the students. They claimed that the stunt gave art a bad name and demanded their money back.

But the 13 students said their holiday – when they swam, sunbathed and visited nightclubs – was designed 'to challenge people's perception of art' and to make people discuss whether there was any limit to what could be described as art.

One of the students, Emma Robertson, said: 'This is leisure as art. It is art and it was an exhibition. People have very set ideas about what art is and we are interested in the media reaction because we want people to discuss what art is.'

About 60 lecturers, local artists and fellow students invited to the first-night party for the exhibition – enigmatically titled Going Places – were surprised when they entered a gallery empty except for a large bowl of sangria, the sound of flamenco music and a drama student dressed as an air hostess with a megaphone.

As they stood around, uncertain what would happen next, they were ushered on to a double-decker bus, driven to Leeds-Bradford airport and left in a bar overlooking the arrivals area. A short time later, they saw the entire troupe of laughing, sun-tanned, third-year students – who had used the money to buy £185 flight-and-accommodation packages – march through Customs armed with souvenirs. The two groups met, the stunt was explained and they all adjourned to the bar again, running up a bill of £180. They spent a couple of hours discussing the meaning of art before they were bussed back to Leeds city centre.

The students' union, which said it had been led to believe that the art students were mounting a more traditional exhibition, suffered a serious humour failure yesterday. Ruth Wilkin, the union's communications officer, said:

'We have asked for the money back. When we gave the money there was no mention of any holidays. We have very limited resources and we are trying to raise £20,000 for a minibus with access for the disabled. It is fairly outrageous and pretty upsetting to see some of our students taking money for a holiday when it should have been spent on a much worthier cause.'

Myles Dutton, who runs the Dixon Bate art shop in Leeds, was one of several commercial sponsors who gave more than £400 for what they thought was a conventional exhibition. He said: 'I gave £50. It's not a lot but I feel I have been duped and I want my money back.'

A university spokesman declined to condemn the students and said: 'It should be noted that on little more than £1,000 they managed to spend a week in Spain, hire a space for the exhibition, hire the double-decker bus and keep a tab behind the bar at the airport. They got a lot out of it.'

The Daily Telegraph

 **COMPREHENSION**

1 How much were the art students given?
2 Where did they go with the money?
3 How did the students justify their trip?
4 What does the article mean by the 'students' union ... suffered a serious humour failure'?
5 Does Myles Dutton want his money back because of the size of his donation?
6 What was the university's reaction to the trip?

DISCUSSION

1 Do you think the students produced a piece of art with their holiday? Why, why not?

2 How would you have felt had you been one of the sponsors?

3 What do you think is the purpose of art?

4 What do you think is good and bad art?

5 Do you think art is necessary, or is it a luxury?

6 Do you think it is important that art pushes the boundaries of taste (see ammunition box)? Why, why not?

7 Do you think art should be censored when it is too shocking? Why, why not?

8 Do you think some modern artists *only* produce works that arouse controversy – thus increasing their fame?

Mother and Child Divided, *winner of the 1995 Turner Prize, Damien Hirst*

"I like it."

ACTIVITIES

A In groups, imagine you are putting on an exhibition of the greatest works of art in the world. You can choose whatever you want up to five pieces.

B ✍ The newspaper that published the article has asked for letters from its readers to express their opinions on what the students did. Write in with your opinion, and what you think should happen next.

 NETWORKING

Find out more about modern art in your country. Who are the most famous artists working at the moment?

Books: *History of Modern Art: Painting, Sculpture, Architecture and Photography* by H. Harvard *The 20th Century Art Book* published by Phaidon

Play: *Art* by Yasmina Reza

Websites:
www.artic.edu/
www.guggenheim.org/solomon
www.louvre.fr/
www.moma.org/
museoprado.mcu.es/
www.nationalgallery.org.uk/
www.uffizi.firenze.it

AMMUNITION BOX

Key words
trend *a style*
masterpiece *an artist's great work*
classic *a unique piece of art*
outrageous *shocking*
fundamental *essential*
shocking *surprising, bad*
avant-garde *experimental, modern*
tasteless *vulgar, unattractive*
movement *a new development in art*
original *something that existed at the beginning of a process*

Handy hints
- The Turner Prize is Britain's most famous art prize and also provokes controversy. The exhibition of finalists attracts crowds of 120,000. The 1999 exhibition contained an exhibit by Tracy Emin, the *enfant terrible* of the British art world. It showed an unmade bed surrounded by champagne corks, used condoms and soiled underwear
- New York mayor Rudolph Giuliani attempted to halt the exhibition 'Sensation: young British artists', on show at the Brooklyn Museum of Art, by withdrawing its subsidy of $497,554. He was particularly shocked by the work *Holy Virgin Mary* by Chris Ofili which is decorated with elephant dung and pornographic images. Other work included Damien Hirst's dead shark floating in a tank of formaldehyde and Mark Quinn's cast of a man's head made from his own frozen blood

 **FOCUS**

- Why do you think people cheat?
- What famous cheats can you think of?

Sport must decide if it really wants a moral stand

by Michael Herd

Ben Johnson v Carl Lewis was billed as The Main Event, an Olympic celebration of human excellence. The black Canadian, born in Jamaica, confirmed he was the fastest man on earth when he sprinted to a gold medal in Seoul. Hours afterwards, we had confirmation that he had chosen to cheat. Two drug tests of Johnson's urine proved positive and he was stripped of his gold, his record and his dignity.

Johnson is trying to have a life ban overturned in the courts. He is suing the Canadian Centre for Ethics in Sport and has alleged an international conspiracy involving the International Olympic Committee, the International Amateur Athletic Federation and the CCES. He claims the majority of athletes at the Seoul Games were on some substance. 'Take the medals away from the East Germans and give them to the Americans? Give me a break!' he says.

Olympic medallists Randy Barnes (shot putt) and Dennis Mitchell (sprint) are suspended by the IAAF for drug violations. Mitchell is chairman of the United States Track and Field's drugs committee. Swimming awaits a drugs verdict on Ireland's Michelle de Bruin, cycling's Tour de France was a farce and we know the Chinese are at it and the East Germans were. A coach claims Italian football has a serious drugs problem. Even worse, Juan Antonio Samaranch, President of the International Olympic Committee, now suggests the list of banned drugs should be greatly reduced.

The IAAF agreed to a serious relaxation of drug laws. An earlier official inquiry concluded that there is a laxity of investigation, a laxity of enforcement and a lack of ethical and moral values.

It is clear that drug-taking is a way of life for many top sportsmen and women. It is obvious that, by condoning the cheating, many administrators, managers and coaches are guilty of conspiracy.

Everything suggests we have finally reached the stage where the sporting world has to make a decision.

If we choose the path of righteousness, then morality and the rules must become one. Sport must tighten regulations, uniformly punishing offenders with life bans.

Conversely, if sporting morality has become just a gesture, then a decision must be made that anything goes.

Some already believe that athletes should be free to do as they please. If that happens, today's cheats will become tomorrow's heroes. We won't give a damn if, like Ben Johnson, they take testosterone to increase muscular size and strength. We won't care if some of our female competitors have chin stubble.

Some athletes will be so frantic to succeed, that they will be prepared to do anything. The youth of that day will fill their bodies with performance-enhancing drugs, ignoring the grave risk of side effects.

I have no doubt that young men and women will die in the pursuit of what they regard as perfection. When the first athlete self-destructs, the sporting world will have to ask how it happened. The answer will be that the fault lies not with the athlete but with the administrators. They will be found guilty of an abdication of authority, of failing to protect athletes from themselves.

They will probably end up in a court of law.

Evening Standard

Ben Johnson

??? COMPREHENSION

1 Who was Ben Johnson's main rival at the Seoul Olympics?
2 What was Johnson's reaction to losing the gold medal?
3 What is ironic about Dennis Mitchell's position?
4 In your own words, state the choice facing sport today.
5 What is the danger of using drugs in sport?
6 Who should we blame if an athlete dies and what will be their fate?

DISCUSSION

1 What do you think about sportsmen and women who take drugs?

2 Is taking drugs cheating, or is it necessary to be able to compete in today's sporting world?

3 Should athletes who take drugs be banned for life? Why, why not? If not, what penalty is suitable?

4 Do you think drugs are used more in sport than 30 years ago?

5 The idea of holding two Olympic Games has been suggested. One where competitors can use drugs, and one where they're banned. What do you think of this idea?

6 Are sports stars cheating in other ways to (see ammunition box)?

7 What do you think could be done to stop drug use and cheating in sport? Educating young sportsmen and women or heavily penalising famous stars to act as a deterrent?

8 Do you think that famous sportsmen and women should also avoid drugs in their private lives? Why, why not?

AMMUNITION BOX

Key words
steroids *drugs that help to build muscle strength*
beta blockers *drugs that help to calm the heart rate, useful to keep steady (sports like shooting)*
banned substance *an illegal drug*
to ban *to say that something must not be used*
suspension *stopping someone from doing something for a period of time*

Handy hints
- During the 1998 Tour de France, three Festina team riders confessed to drug taking
- At Wimbledon in 1998, the tennis player Petr Korda tested positive for steroids, but managed to avoid a ban saying he had no idea how the banned substance nandrolone came to be in his body
- The International Olympic Committee is putting new sanctions in place against any competitor caught taking drugs. The first step will be suspension, and any return to the sport will be monitored on a daily basis. The athlete might also have to pay a fine of up to $1 million
- Two brothers ran a race in South Africa, winning a cash prize, swapping places regularly along the route. They were only discovered when pictures showed one brother wearing a watch on the right wrist, and the other wearing a watch on his left!

NETWORKING

Find out more about drug use in sport and the attitude of the International Olympic Committee.

Books: *Addicted* by Tony Adams
Bodyline by Paul Wheeler
Drugs in Sport by D.R. Mottram, Sally Gunnell
Drugs, Sport and Politics by Robert Voy, Deeter Kirk
Hero & Villain by Paul Merson

Film: *Chariots of Fire* (1981) directed by Hugh Hudson

Websites:
www.iaaf.org/
www.olympic.org/
www.sydney.olympic.org

ACTIVITIES

A Role-play: In groups, imagine you work for the drug-testing agency. Sally Gates, a world champion swimmer, has tested positive for banned steroids. She is a hero in your country, the first person to win a swimming gold for 32 years. Any publicity will be bad for the sport, and will lead to a loss of funding from the government, and you need every penny you can get! It's possible she took the drug accidentally, but there was such a high trace, you think this unlikely. You need to make a decision, and think of any implications.

- Keep quiet and hope no one hears about it
- Call her in for an interview
- Impose a ban upon her

B ✍ The newspaper that printed the article opposite is asking for responses from its readers. Write in with your opinion as to the changes in sport, and what should happen to cheats, and drug users in particular. Be prepared to justify your opinions!

FOCUS

Talking Point: Are beauty contests outdated?

Should the world of beauty pageants remain a kitsch memory firmly stuck in the past, or is it time we learned to love Miss World again?

Well reach for your tiaras and remote controls because it is back.

After a ten year absence from UK terrestrial television, the new and improved Miss World contest is hitting the screens of Channel Five on Thursday.

The new politically correct version has ditched the national costumes, skimpy swimsuits and high heels of old – this year's contestants will be seen in a 'more natural environment' relaxing in jeans and T-shirts. But in sanitising the contest are the organisers removing the meat-market factor or simply being prudes? Why is there no Mr World contest?

Critics are inclined to pan the pageant as an excuse for people to leer at semi-naked women, judging them on their looks and figure alone.

But this year's Miss Malaysia thinks the contest has moved on.

'I think everyone is going to be surprised at how spectacular the event is going to be and how down to earth it is, and they're really making an effort to move into the 21st century,' she said.

Founder of Miss World, Eric Morley, said broadcasters had been foolish to drop the annual ritual.

'People love a competition and when it comes to beauty everyone's an expert,' he said. 'They like to watch Miss World and say "Why did she win? My wife's better looking than her".'

What do you think?

Votes: Yes 7%   No 93%

Beauty pageants are harmless, eh? Then why do so many young girls starve themselves to live up to a ridiculous ideal that these pageants promote and celebrate? I don't think that one can ban them, but at the very least, throw some normal-sized people in there.
Kristen Nicolaisen, USA

Beauty contests are outdated because it is in the eye of the beholder and the contests are meaningless. Also, how can it be Miss World when only 86 out of 191 countries take part? I get the feeling that they try to emphasise beauty as white, or not too dark.
Yoel Sano, UK

Of course not, if over a billion people watch the contest clearly it is not outdated. The argument that it exploits women is absurd. The contestants willingly take part, enjoy it and hope it will provide lucrative careers in fashion or modelling. Feminists need to be reminded that feminists do not own the contestants' bodies and therefore don't need feminist permission to participate.
David Gordon, UK

Beauty contests can serve no real purpose in the fast moving modern world where women have started to drift away from their stereotypical portrayal as sex objects.
RKR, India

Beauty contests are not outdated because it's simply human nature to look at beautiful people. In fact, when it comes to the level of Miss World or Miss Universe, pageants can promote cultural exchange. I sincerely believe not too many people have heard of many of the smaller countries represented at these contests. Besides, how many young people can have a genuine opportunity to travel and be a representative of his/her own country like the participants of Miss World do?
Carter Kwong, Canada

BBC Online

 **COMPREHENSION**

1 Is Miss World returning to television?
2 How is the new version different?
3 Why is Miss World popular according to its founder, Eric Morley?
4 Explain what Yoel Sano means by beauty 'is in the eye of the beholder'.
5 What benefits might contestants get after taking part in beauty contests?
6 Explain how beauty pageants promote cultural exchange.

👥 DISCUSSION

1 Which of the speakers do you agree with most? Were any points made that you particularly agree/disagree with?

2 What effect do you think beauty competitions have on the contestants?

3 Do you know of any beauty competitions for men? Are they different in any way?

4 Do different countries and cultures have different ideas of beauty, or is there a common ideal of world beauty?

5 Do you think beauty contests are biased towards women of a certain race?

6 Do you think beauty contests are outdated? Why, why not?

7 Do you think beauty competitions such as Miss World are demeaning or insulting to women? Why, why not?

🌐 NETWORKING

Find out more about beauty contests all over the world. What kinds of people enter, and how popular are they? Would you enter?

Book: *The Beauty Myth* by Naomi Wolf

Film: *Drop Dead Gorgeous* (1999) directed by Michael Patrick Jann

Video: *Investigative Reports – Beauty Pageants: Bright Lights, Big Business* (1994)

Websites:
pageantcenter.com/history.html
www.beautycontestinfo.com/index.htm

🏃 ACTIVITIES

A Role-play: In groups, imagine you are a team of producers for a TV channel. Recently it has been suggested that a beauty competition might be a good way of attracting more viewers. You need to think about:

- The rules of the competition
- Who can enter (men or women)
- The prize
- What the contestants will wear
- How you will make your contest different in order to attract viewers

When you have finished, present and compare your ideas with those of other groups in the class. Who has the best proposal?

B ✍ Write a response to the article.

Or

✍ Write up your proposal for the directors of the TV channel. Explain to them what the programme is and why you think it will be successful (you need them to back this project).

Miss World 1998

🧨 AMMUNITION BOX

Key words
fair *honest*
contestants *people who take part in a competition*
approach *the way of dealing with something*
equality *the state of being equal*
outdated *old-fashioned*
chauvinistic *when men believe they are better than women*

Handy hints
- In the southern USA, child beauty pageants are very popular. Children dress up in specially designed outfits (that can cost hundreds of dollars). These pageants often involve singing and dancing routines (singing adult songs), and prizes can range up to $25,000. The entry age can be as low as one year old!
- In beauty contest mad Venezuela virtually the whole country tunes in. So popular are beauty queens that an ex-Miss World even ran for the presidential nomination. Venezuela has developed various beauty competitions, including one for grannies and another for women in prison!
- A 'beauty' competition of a different kind takes place in England. At the world 'gurning' competition the male competitors will pull the most hideous face they can, and the ugliest is declared the winner!

- What do you think is the purpose of prison?
- Are there any alternatives to prison?

'I love my electronic ball and chain'

Mina is one of the first prisoners to be tagged electronically. But life under constant curfew is better than jail.

Two weeks ago, Mina's home was a prison. Today she is sitting in her living room. The slim, grey band encircling her left ankle holds the key to her freedom. Mina is one of 1,500 prisoners who are currently being monitored under the Government's Home Detention Curfew (HDC).

Under the system, offenders are placed under a home curfew and are fitted with an electronic tag which sends signals to monitoring equipment installed in their homes. If the conditions are broken, the signal will alert the authorities.

HDC aims to provide 'a managed transition between prison and living in the community'. The curfew times and boundaries are prearranged with the prison governor and can be tailored to individual needs. Mina must be indoors from 7pm to 7am but has a special extension to go to night classes once a week.

Around 60,000 prisoners will be eligible for HDC, and it is estimated that half that number will pass the risk assessment necessary to take part in the scheme. This will result in around 4,000 of the 65,000 prison population being tagged at any one time.

Mina claims she had to fight tooth and nail for her freedom, and now she is free Mina is a fan of the system. 'It is wonderful to be back in my home again – I don't miss going out in the evenings. I have the freedom to look for work, run my house and look after my dog.'

The Home Office insists that the scheme is tamper-proof, but there have been cases of offenders slipping their tags. 'Girls in prison used to boast that they would cut their tags off when they got outside, that's really stupid. It would be a shame if it was ruined for everybody else.'

Although Mina has no intention of breaking her curfew, accidents can happen. 'One evening I'd allowed myself two hours to drive back from Central London but the traffic was bumper to bumper. I had to break the speed limit to get back. I flung myself through the door – tagged ankle first – and made it with 30 seconds to spare.'

The Home Office says the system is designed to cope with emergencies and the occasional mishap, but repeated violations of the curfew would result in the offender returning to jail.

Mina says that she does not feel particularly stigmatised by the tag. 'It's nobody's business but mine, although I don't advertise the fact that I'm wearing it'

The Big Issue

COMPREHENSION

1 Where on her body does Mina wear her tag?
2 How many prisoners are being monitored?
3 Is Mina positive about the scheme?
4 What is Mina worried about? Why?
5 How does the Home Office say the system will manage violations?

AMMUNITION BOX

Key words
to **discipline** *to train or control*
penalty *punishment for breaking the law*
punitive *very severe, harsh*
to **authorise** *to give approval, permission for something*
selection *the process of choosing something carefully*
redemptive *improved or saved*

Handy hints
- In May 1998 the prison population in England and Wales was 65,519
- A total of 4,807 offenders have been tagged since the trial started in July 1995
- 1,886 are still being monitored
- 215 orders have been revoked, 4% of the total
- The study has cost £3 million

Leeds Prison, England

ACTIVITIES

A Role-play: You are the governors of Mina's prison. You have four candidates for the Home Detention Curfew scheme (HDC), but can only accept one of them. In groups of two or three, discuss who you would chose, and be prepared to justify your choice to the class.

Name: Cynthia Dale

Age: 45

Crime: Murder

Sentence: Life

Notes: Ms Dale is a quiet, shy woman. She was convicted of murdering her husband after suffering years of abuse. Her husband's family have said they oppose her release in any way.

Name: Barbara McHeath

Age: 33

Crime: Armed Robbery

Sentence: 10 years

Notes: Although Ms McHeath appears a kind woman, she took part in a violent robbery. However, she is in poor health and doctors think she might die if kept in prison.

Name: Annie Lake

Age: 55

Crime: Theft

Sentence: 5 years

Notes: Ms Lake lives alone and has no family. In prison she has been a model prisoner and has caused no discipline problems. She is very keen to get onto the scheme.

Name: Diane Moor

Age: 21

Crime: Fraud

Sentence: 7 years

Notes: Divorcee Ms Moor was found guilty of taking £500,000 from her work. She has now lost everything, and has asked to be put on the scheme so that she can look after her three young children. She has caused some discipline problems.

B There are other ways that governments could try to reduce overcrowding.
For example, in England there is a prison ship moored off Dorset. Write an essay about possible ways of tackling overcrowding in prisons.

DISCUSSION

1 What are the advantages of HDC?

2 Do you think it is right to let prisoners out on a scheme like this?

3 Do you think prison is a place for punishment, rehabilitation, or both?

4 How would you feel about Mina if you saw her with her tag on the street?

5 How do you think you would feel wearing one of these tags?

6 What is the attitude of your society to prison? Do you agree with it?

7 Do you think more people should be imprisoned for their crimes, or should more alternatives like HDC be found?

8 Look at the graph showing the prison population in the UK. Can you think of ways to reduce overcrowding in prisons?

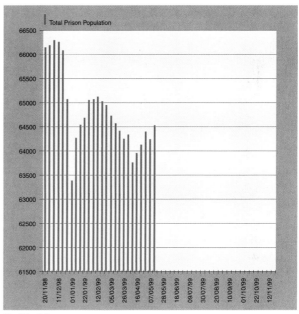

Prison Reform Trust

NETWORKING

Find out about prisons in your country. Is there a problem of overcrowding?

Books: *A Man in Full* (Prison Section) by Tom Wolfe
Crime and Punishment by Fyodor Dostoevsky
Long Walk to Freedom: The Autobiography by Nelson Mandela
The Ballad of Reading Gaol by Oscar Wilde
The Oxford History of the Prison by Morris, Norval and Rothman, D.J.

Films: *Dead Man Walking* (1995) directed by Tim Robbins
In The Name Of The Father (1993) directed by Jim Sheridan
Papillon (1973) directed by Franklin J. Schaffner
The Shawshank Redemption (1994) directed by Frank Darabont

Websites: www.homeoffice.gov.uk/
www.open.gov.uk/

The UK has some of the most congested roads in the world.
- What do you think are some of the consequences of traffic congestion?
- What are some alternatives to the car?

Experts fear start of 'road rage' trend

by **Don Russell**, Daily News Staff Writer

The local traffic report is starting to sound like the police blotter

On Aug. 3, while trying to park his car on South Street, a 23-year-old West Philly man was shot in the head by another driver who wanted the spot.

A week later, an argument between the occupants of two cars on Allegheny Avenue erupted into gunfire. A 19-year-old woman was shot in the head.

On Aug. 12, the driver of a sport-utility vehicle tried to run a van driver off the road in Upper Darby. After a collision, the first driver stabbed the second in the leg.

How long till we have to buckle up both our safety belts and our bulletproof vests when we climb behind the wheel?

Police say incidents like these – known as road rage – are still rare in the Philadelphia area. But traffic experts are worried we may be seeing the beginning of a far more deadly trend.

'It's going to get worse,' said Leon James, a University of Hawaii traffic psychology professor known as Dr. Driving.

James and others believe violent highway incidents are merely extreme examples of our everyday aggressive driving behavior. The Daily News reported last month that drivers who have abandoned civil roadway behavior are causing about half of all serious traffic accidents.

'Tailgating, running red lights, speeding and hazardous lane changes are common behavior on the highway,' said James.

'Aggressive driving is not extreme any more; it has become a cultural norm on the highway,' James said.

And it's going to get worse for two big reasons, experts say. First, traffic is becoming more congested. That means drivers have more opportunities to engage in violent encounters. Second, we are a violent society that is proud, not ashamed, of aggressive behavior.

What's going to reverse the trend? Earlier this month, the National Conference of State Legislatures tackled that question during its annual meeting in Philadelphia. Some legislators – though none from Pennsylvania or New Jersey – said they had tried to introduce new laws that outlaw aggressive driving. None have been adopted so far because lawmakers have been unable to define aggressive driving. But Carol Petzhold, a Maryland legislature delegate, insisted, 'You and I know what aggressive driving is when we see it.'

Other experts believe the problem can be solved with enforcement of existing laws. That's the cornerstone of a new program in the Washington, D.C., area called Smooth Operator. Police initiated the program after a 80mph road duel on the George Washington Parkway killed three people. In its first two weeks, Smooth Operator ticketed more than 27,000 drivers for speeding, tailgating, improper passing and failure to obey signals. By comparison, the Daily News has found that Philadelphia police rarely write tickets for aggressive driving. For instance, in 1995, police wrote 137 tickets for red-light running, which is the city's No. 1 cause of accidents.

Though experts say increased law enforcement is a big part of the solution, psychologists like James say the problem runs even deeper into the soul of our violent nation.

'We're born into road rage; we inherit it from our parents,' said James. 'We acquire it automatically as children from adult drivers, cartoons, television, and commercials. Every driver at some point has these violent thoughts against another driver,' he continued. 'There's a Jekyll and Hyde transformation when we get behind the wheel of a car. The car is our castle and the road is our freedom. When somebody gets in the way of it, we get hostile,' James said.

For James, the solution is better driver education that stresses the ability to contain hostility and to avoid disputes. 'If we don't do something, these violent incidents are going to get worse,' James said. 'What's increasing is our acceptance of road rage, our self-righteous indignation about other drivers. People feel almost proud of their aggressiveness.'

The Philadelphia Daily News

AMMUNITION BOX

Key words
road rage *drivers become so aggressive they physically attack one another*
to subsidise *the government gives money to support certain groups or organisations so that they can keep their prices low*
congestion *roads are too crowded*
pollution *the environment is made dirty by harmful substances, such as car fumes*
aggressive *behaving in a hostile or violent way*
verbal abuse *someone attacks you by shouting*

Handy hints
Various countries have tried different ways to cut down on traffic:
- In Singapore it is necessary to buy a Certificate of Entitlement (COE) before being able to buy a car, and the price can be thousands of dollars. Road pricing also applies to key roads at busy times, but the island enjoys an excellent public transport infrastructure
- In Holland there are excellent cycleways all over the country
- Research by the AA (Automobile Association) found that 90% of motorists had encountered road rage and that 60% admitted losing their temper while driving
- Road rage is more common in cities, with 44% of motorists claiming to have been victims in the past 12 months

COMPREHENSION

1 What was the first road rage incident?
2 Are road rage incidents common in Philadelphia?
3 Is road rage seen as extreme behaviour?
4 What reasons do psychologists put forward for road rage?

Why pedalling is heart to beat

By Philip Douglas

Britain would be healthier and wealthier if more people got on their bikes. Not only would roads be less congested and less polluted, but cyclists would be fitter and could expect a longer life. Mike Collins from cycling charity Sustrans says: 'A cyclist of 50 would have the health of a 40-year-old.'

The Health Education Authority says that cycling for as little as half an hour a day – a journey of about five miles – can halve the risk of heart disease. Longer term, cycling could also help avert one of the great threats of the age – global warming. Taking to two wheels is pollution free.

The other great benefit is that cycling is cheap. So it's hardly surprising that each year more trips are made by bike than by train and London Underground combined. But Britain's 20 million bicycles need to be put to regular use. Then they can be of really effective benefit to everyone – even non-cyclists.

The Express

COMPREHENSION

1 What are the benefits of cycling?
2 What environmental benefits does cycling have?
3 Do people use London Underground more than they use their bikes?
4 How do you think cycling could avert global warming?

ACTIVITIES

A Role-play: Imagine you are a member of the council for your local city. The traffic problem there has become almost unbearable. The roads are carrying about 20% more traffic than they were designed for. It is your job to come up with a solution to the traffic congestion and present it to the public. There are pros and cons with each solution, so you need to consider the problem carefully.

Note: You are up for election in six months time. Does that affect your decision?

What will your solution be? Choose possible solutions and try to think of alternatives.

B ✍ Write an essay: Ways to stop road rage.

Or

✍ Write a letter to the newspaper about a road rage incident that happened to you – invent any details.

• **Build more cycle routes.** [This would mean a cleaner less congested environment. However, there would be less space for cars and parking. The cycling lobby and environmental groups support this.]

• **Tax cars locally.** [This would discourage people from buying cars and free revenue to spend on other projects. However, the business community has objected and threatened to leave the city should this happen, politically very unpopular.]

• **Subsidise local transport.** [Increase bus and train routes, consider re-introducing trams. This would make public transport cheaper and easier. However, higher taxes to pay for it may prove politically unpopular.]

• **Build more roads.** [This is what business leaders are asking for. It won't solve the problem long term, and will only encourage more cars, increase pollution and destroy the countryside. Unpopular with environmentalists.]

DISCUSSION

1 Have you ever suffered from road rage? What happened?

2 Why do you think drivers become so aggressive when other cars get in their way?

3 Do you think people would be calmer if they cycled? If so, why?

4 How popular is cycling in your country? What could be done to encourage cycling?

5 Do you think society is becoming more accepting of violence? Why, why not?

6 Should any limits be placed on car ownership? If so, how? By increasing taxes, limiting the number of cars per household?

7 What or who do you think is the most dangerous – cars, car drivers or other road users? Give your reasons.

8 How do you travel to the following places: school or work, a shopping centre, a nightclub with friends? Could you use another mode of transport to any of these?

9 How do you think people could become less aggressive?

NETWORKING

Find out about road rage incidence in your country. What other things lead to violent public outrage? What do you feel rage about? Does violence do any good ?

Book: *Gridlock* by Ben Elton

Websites:
www.roads.detr.gov.uk
www.tcsu.org.uk/

15

FOCUS

- Is there a drug problem in your country?
- Are people punished for drug use?

The Coffee Shop Situation

In 1976, Holland decided that the crime around selling drugs was a greater threat than the health problem caused to the drug user. So to separate marijuana from the underworld, they decriminalized it and cannabis became tolerated – but not technically legalized – by the government. Respectable coffee-shop owners cheered this approach and welcomed the stability and security of being legitimate, even if it meant paying more taxes.

The Parool, Amsterdam's leading newspaper, asked the mayor how much a gram of marijuana costs in his city. 'f15 a gram,' he answered. In other countries people would be surprised the mayor knows how much a bag of weed is, but in Holland, the man shaping an intelligent drug policy knows the facts.

Meanwhile, the rest of the world continues its unending 'war on drugs'. French President Jacques Chirac blamed

Teenager smoking marijuana

Holland for its drug troubles, even though, according to Time magazine, Holland has fewer addicts per thousand than France and supplies fewer drugs to France than Spain, Pakistan and Morocco.

This year it was the U.S. drug-czar Barry McCaffery who came to celebrate America's successful drug policy. Although one may have expected him to be curious about coffee shops here, he found no need to visit one because it was a 'bad photo opportunity.'

He went further, calling Holland's progressive drug policy 'an unmitigated disaster', citing higher crime in Holland as proof. Huh? I don't know what he smokes, but this country is safe, and there is no place in the western world with more violence than America. But I guess when you're fighting a 'war', the truth sometimes has to be suppressed.

So in a bow to foreign pressure, the government reduced the amount of soft drugs an individual can possess from 30 grams to five. But maybe Holland should go further. If they recriminalize drugs, maybe they can wipe them out altogether, just like France and America.

While we're at it, maybe France can give us some advice on how to end strikes and reduce unemployment, and the U.S. about stopping violence in schools.

No matter what happens in the long run, you can still go into any 'coffee shop', proudly march up to the bartender, and announce in a loud voice: 'I want to buy some hashish, and then I'm going to smoke it.' Most places will even have rolling papers and filter tips on the bar.

There are several types of hash and pot, which have been bred to produce different highs. Each coffee shop has its own name for its weed, even if it comes from the same place. Just don't let the big menu scare you. (Yes, they'll have a menu.)

Hash comes in two basic varieties: blond and black. The black hash hits a little harder and knocks you out a little more. Locals smoke the lighter stuff.

Any place that calls itself a 'coffee shop' is saying three things: 1) I have pot and hash for you to buy. 2) For the price of a coffee or beer, you may sit here and smoke your own as well. 3) You may also smoke on my outdoor terrace, even in front of the police.

Boom!

COMPREHENSION

1 What happened in 1976?
2 Why does the mayor know how much a gram of marijuana costs?
3 Explain what is meant by a 'bad photo opportunity'.
4 The writer uses a lot of irony in his piece. Find an example, and explain why it's ironic.
5 What facilities do the coffee shops have for the marijuana user?

DISCUSSION

1 The author seems to think a relaxed approach to the drugs problem is best – do you agree with him? Why, why not?

2 Do you think drugs are more acceptable now than a generation ago?

3 Why do you think people are drawn to taking drugs?

4 Do you think there's a relationship between drug use and crime? Give details.

5 In terms of the law, should a difference be made between those who use so-called soft drugs, such as marijuana, and those who use hard drugs like cocaine and heroin? Why, why not?

6 Do you think use of soft drugs inevitably leads to use of heroin and cocaine? Why, why not?

7 Do you think there should be any difference made between those who use drugs and those who sell drugs, and what would be a suitable punishment in each case?

8 Which policy do you agree with most – zero tolerance, as is the case in America, or the more relaxed attitude in Holland? Why?

9 Do you think drugs can ever be completely wiped out? Why, why not?

ACTIVITIES

A Role-play. In groups of four or five. Your country has recently seen a big increase in drug use amongst the young. The government – after looking at the different approaches of Holland and New York – has called on your committee to produce a range of ideas to lead the fight against the drugs menace. Together, you need to think about:

- New laws, whether to penalise drug use/the drug trade OR to legalise certain aspects of it (give details about these laws)
- How best to educate the public against the dangers posed by drugs
- Any other measures you think might be effective in the war against drugs

B ✍ Write up your ideas on fighting drugs as a report for the government. Outline the problem, what measures you think are needed to combat it and why.

Or

✍ Write a letter to the magazine that published the article. Give your opinion of what's happening in Holland, and in any other country that you know. State what you think are the best solutions to the drug problem, and why.

AMMUNITION BOX

Key words
zero tolerance *the policy of punishing someone, even for a minor offence*
decriminalise *to make something legal*
to eradicate *to get rid of something*
recreational use *using drugs occasionally, to relax, not an addict*
addicted to *when you cannot give something up*
intravenous *injecting drugs into a vein*
to educate *to inform*

Handy hints
- Penalties for carrying marijuana in America

Quantity	First offence	Second offence
Less than 50 kg	not more than five years	not more than 10 years
50-99 kg	not less than 20 years	not more than 30 years
100-999 kg	not less than five years	not less than 10 years
1,000 kg or more	not less than 10 years	not less than 20 years

- Cost to society*
  – People in prison due to drug-related crime: 20.4% of the prison population
  – Costs from premature deaths: 14.9% of the general population
  – Lost productivity due to drug-related illness: 14.5% of the general population
- Between 1988 and 1995, Americans spent $57.3 billion on drugs
  $38 billion on cocaine
  $9.6 billion on heroin
  $7 billion on marijuana
  $2.7 billion on other illegal drugs

*Source: National Institute of Drug Abuse

NETWORKING

Find out more about drug use in your country.
How widespread is it, and how are people who use drugs punished?

Books: *Bright Lights, Big City* by Jay McInerney
Mr Nice by Howard Marks
Trainspotting by Irvine Welsh

Film: *Fear and Loathing in Las Vegas* (1998) directed by Terry Gilliam
Trainspotting (1996) by Danny Boyle

Websites:
www.ecad.net/
www.ojp.usdoj.gov/bjs/drugs.htm

FOCUS

- What was the last item of clothing you bought? How much did you spend?
- How important are clothes to you?

What is your wardrobe worth?

Rachida Addou, 22, heiress. Cost of wardrobe: £500,000

I don't like to be seen in the same dress more than once, so I have more than 30 ball gowns and evening dresses. I'll pay anything up to £20,000 for a dress. I keep most of my dresses, which together are worth about £200,000, at our house in Spain.

Dresses are my favourite items of clothing. For my wedding in September next year, I've had seven designed for me. The celebrations will last three days, so apart from the white dress for the ceremony, the rest are ball gowns and evening dresses of every colour under the sun. I can't wait to get married. Because of the nature of my fiancé's job we'll always be away. I don't work – and won't work. I spend my days shopping.

My day wardrobe comprises mainly Valentino, Dolce & Gabbana and Georges Rech. I own five outfits from each designer. Accessories have to be either Christian Dior or Chanel. Some of my bags cost £700, the others thousands. For best value, you can't beat Louis Vuitton. The leather is exquisite. I also have a few Gucci wallets and sunglasses. Shoes are my other weakness. I pay about £300 for a pair of shoes.

My jewellery must be worth the same as my clothes. Most of it's Cartier, including a diamond-encrusted watch and ring my parents gave me last summer. It wasn't even a birthday present – more of a pre-wedding gift.

Roz Barnett, 27, Lance Corporal in the army. Cost of wardrobe: £1,000

It's pretty fortunate that I'm not into fashion – at all. Being in the army gives me little opportunity to dress up in civilian clothes. Most women would be horrified by the contents of my two wardrobes. I have one at the barracks, in Aldershot, Hampshire, for my uniform, and another for my civilian gear. I live in T-shirts, tracksuits and trainers when not in army gear. I have four pairs of trainers and three tracksuits and that's about it. I do own one or two smart items. The last dress I bought – for Christmas, over a year ago – was a purple evening gown. It was the most expensive thing I've ever splashed out on – £35, from Next. I refuse to spend more.

I live five days a week in my uniform combat gear; khaki-coloured combat trousers and shirt, boots and a maroon beret. I also have a dress uniform, which is worn on occasions like Remembrance Day. It's a rather attractive A-line khaki-coloured suit, which I wear with a cream blouse, khaki tie, black tights and flat, shiny, lace-up shoes. Oh, and we have our physical training gear.

Make-up and hair have to be 'non-distinctive'. Women can wear foundation and mascara, but nothing else. Long hair has to be worn up, under the beret. No jewellery either, apart from a wedding ring and plain ear studs.

I've never missed not being able to wear civilian clothes all week, even when I was 18. The joy of a uniform is that you never have to think about what to wear in the morning – or spend lots of money on clothes.

Marie Claire

COMPREHENSION

1 How much does Rachida pay for a dress?
2 Are trousers Rachida's favourite clothing?
3 Who are her favourite designers?
4 Does Roz spend a lot on clothes?
5 What clothes does she wear during the week?
6 What was the most expensive item Roz ever bought?
7 What are the advantages of wearing a uniform?

DISCUSSION

1 Which woman's attitude to clothes is closest to your own?

2 What is your reaction to the prices Rachida is happy to pay for her clothes?

3 Do you think there is something immoral in paying so much for a dress when so many people can't afford to eat?

4 Do you think designer goods – such as Gucci, Chanel and Dior – are worth the money, or are you paying for the name?

5 Do you follow fashion trends closely? Why, why not?

6 Do you think women spend more on shopping than men? What things do men spend more on?

7 Do you think people judge others by the clothes they wear? Why, why not?

ACTIVITIES

A **Debate the issue: You are what you wear.**

B ✍ **Write an account similar to the article about the contents of your wardrobe.**
If you wish to keep your clothes a secret or make your wardrobe more interesting, invent the details!
Or

✍ **Write a letter to one of the women in the article telling her what you think about her attitude towards clothes.**

NETWORKING

Find out about the fashion industry in your country.

Books: *Coco Chanel and Chanel* by David Bond
Gianni Versace by Richard Martin
The End of Fashion: The Mass Marketing of the Clothing Business by Terri Agins

Film: *Pret à Porter* (1994) by Robert Altman

TV: *Absolutely Fabulous*

Websites:
click.hotbot.co
www.fashion.net/
www.harrods.com
www.vogue.com

AMMUNITION BOX

Key words
to exploit *to take advantage of*
to show off *to show something you have that others will want*
snobbery *the feeling of being better than others, usually because you are rich*
extravagant *spending a lot of money on things that are not necessary*
haute-couture *high quality fashion clothes*
designer label *an item of clothing designed by a top designer*
exterior *someone's appearance*
superficial *not thinking, feeling deeply*

Handy hints
- Calvin Klein is one of the fashion world's biggest names. *Time* magazine lists him as one of America's 25 most influential people. He is well-known for his advertising campaigns, and caused a storm of controversy when he featured a teenage Brooke Shields with the slogan 'You know what comes between me and my Calvin's? Nothing.'
- Giorgio Armani is one of Italy's best-known names. The Armani empire consists of 2,000 *Emporia* shops and has annual sales of more than $1 billion.
- Yves Saint Laurent is famous for having created the 'Beat Look' in the 60s. He is credited with having introduced the trouser suit into women's fashion. In 1985 he was decorated with a Knighthood of the Legion of Honour by President François Mitterrand. In 1995 he was promoted to the rank of Officer of the Legion of Honour.

- How much AIDS awareness and education is there in your country?
- What is the typical view of religious organisations to AIDS?

Church doctrine barrier to Pacific fight against Aids

> 'The epidemic is far from over. The crisis is actually growing.'
>
> Dr Peter Piot
> UN Agency executive director

The Rev Lotu Uele preaches the word of God in the villages of Samoa, but in conflict with his church's doctrine he also promotes the use of condoms to fight the deadly virus that causes AIDS.

'I support the use of condoms to prevent Aids. If this is the way of protecting people from Aids, why shouldn't we promote its use?' said a defiant Uele, from the Congregational Church of Samoa.

But Uele is one of few clerics in the deeply religious South Pacific willing to break the taboo of confronting the spectre of Aids.

Missionaries have historically led the fight against disease on the coral-fringed islands where cultural taboos, particularly regarding sex, often hinder modern medicine.

But today, churches are reluctant to become involved in the new medical battle because they fear being seen to promote adultery and homosexuality, both anathema to church doctrine. Health workers say the fight against Aids in the islands cannot be won without the support of churches and their traditional village network.

Tongan Princess Alaile'ula Tuku'aho told the South Pacific's first Aids conference in Fiji that she was angry at allegations that some churches were not

practising Christian principles of love, care and compassion towards Aids sufferers.

The Princess called on South Pacific churches to drop their prejudices against HIV and Aids patients and lead the fight.

'As a Christian I was brought up to believe that providing care and support for the sick and suffering, irrespective of the cause of the sickness, is one of the most fundamental roles of the Church,' she said. 'We all look forward to hearing how we can assist the churches in our countries to play a more active role in creating the caring and non-judgmental environment required by people living with HIV-Aids.'

Dr Rob Moodie, head of the Victorian Health Promotions Foundation in Australia and a long-time Aids fighter, told the conference that South Pacific churches had the power to change deep community prejudices towards sufferers.

'As the Church is a powerful influence in the region, its embrace of the issue of HIV-Aids impacts significantly on the wider community,

acting to shift people's perceptions about the virus,' Moodie said.

He praised Uele and other clerics for their public stance. But he added: 'No doubt you have been criticised by some of your colleagues and some of your parishioners for your commitment to HIV-Aids.'

Mountainous, densely jungled Papua New Guinea (PNG) has been the hardest-hit country in the South Pacific, producing the region's highest per capita HIV and Aids infection rate.

The World Health Organisation has warned that PNG is on the verge of a combined HIV-tuberculosis epidemic of 'African proportions' and has identified PNG and its population of just over four million as one of seven Asia-Pacific hotspots.

But the sex taboo remains the big barrier to stopping the spread of HIV and Aids.

'Sex is a word that many of us do not like to talk about,' said Dr Clement Malau from the Secretariat of the Pacific Community in Noumea. 'I believe one of our greatest challenges is how we need to talk more freely and openly about sex ... so informed sustainable decisions can be made by individuals and communities.'

New Zealand Herald

COMPREHENSION

1 Does the Rev Lotu Uele support the use of condoms?
2 Does the church support him? Why, why not?
3 How does Tongan Princess Alaile'ula Tuku'aho see the duty of good Christians?
4 What does Dr Rob Moodie think the church can do?
5 Papua New Guinea has the most HIV/AIDS sufferers in the South Pacific – true or false? Justify your answer.
6 Why is it important to talk more openly about sex in the fight against AIDS?

 DISCUSSION

1 How much of a danger do you think AIDS is to society? Why?

2 Do you think the church is justified in ignoring AIDS sufferers? Why, why not?

3 How are HIV/AIDS sufferers viewed by your society? How can we improve that image?

4 How do you think we can best fight AIDS? What sort of role should the government and religious organisations have?

5 Should research for AIDS be carried out by private drugs companies or international governments? Think of advantages and disadvantages for each.

6 Do you think a cure will ever be found for AIDS?

7 Do you know of other diseases that pose a threat to society?

NETWORKING

Find out about the attitude towards AIDS in your country. What treatments are available? Are there any campaigns that make people aware of the dangers?

Books: *AIDS & HIV in Perspective: A Guide to Understanding the Virus & its Consequences* by Barry Shaub

Film: *KIDS* (1995) directed by Larry Clark *Philadelphia* (1993) directed by Jonathan Demme

Websites:
nat.org.uk
www.tht.org.uk/
www.who.int

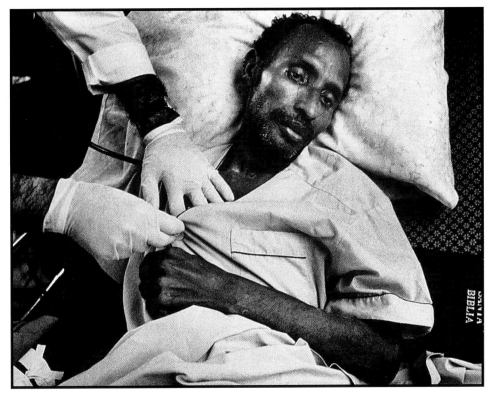
AIDS patient

ACTIVITIES

A Role-play: Imagine you are a group of publicity consultants. The government has asked you to come up with a publicity campaign to make people more aware of AIDS. Think about the following:

- Your target audience
- How you will present your message. Will it shock or frighten people?
- Will you use the latest research figures?
- Will you focus on safe-sex issues?

B ✍ Write an essay: In order to combat diseases such as AIDS, people need to be as open as possible and overcome any taboos. Discuss.

AMMUNITION BOX

Key words
discrimination *treating one group in an unfair way*
treatment *to help cure an injury or illness*
phobia *an unreasonable fear of something*
prejudice *an unreasonable dislike and distrust of people*
complacency *a feeling of self-satisfaction*
realistic *to deal with a situation in a practical way*
open *honest*
frank *truthful*

Handy hints
- 50% of all HIV cases are in southern and eastern Africa. In 1998, 1.4 million people died of AIDS in that region. Average life expectancy is expected to fall from 60 to 40
- AIDS is also the major cause of death for women aged between 20 and 40 in North and South America
- Treatment can cost $15,000 per patient. 90% of infections happen in the developing world, where budgets can be as low as $10 per patient
- Drugs companies are charged with putting profit before patients

21

- How well is food labelled in your country?
- What do you know about genetically modified (GM) food?

Food labelling too much to swallow

'**BACON** on a bun with lettuce and tomato, please. But hold the human, scorpion and flounder bits ...'

Genetically engineered food is in every meal we eat. Unless you're a strictly organic vegetarian, you have already ingested vast quantities of ordinary staples (soya, potatoes, fruits and vegetables) juiced up with assorted viruses, bacteria and other toxins that have never been tested for long-term safety.

True, you're not actually chewing down on scorpions when some of their genetic material has been cleverly introduced into a vegetable. But wouldn't you like to have a choice?

When you peer at the fine print while trying to shop

conscientiously, wouldn't you appreciate knowing that the No fat! condiment you're about to buy is loaded with extra sugar? Right now, the label doesn't have to breathe a word about any of the less desirable elements lurking in the food.

What a contrast to Britain, where a sizzling campaign by consumers has forced major grocery chains and packagers to renounce genetically modified (GM) foods entirely. Prompted by an outraged public, the European Union has already rejected genetically altered crops from North America and insisted on distinctive marking of GM packaged foods.

It's our turn now, if we care to take it. Maybe Canadians have finally learned we can't take public safety for granted. Two new campaigns are under way: The Alliance for Food Label Reform is lobbying for compulsory nutrition labelling, and the Council of Canadians will soon begin a push to label all genetically altered foods. Both organizations have rafts of persuasive evidence.

The alliance points out that 86 to 90 per cent of Canadians consistently tell pollsters that they want clear nutritional labelling.

After all, our grocery ignorance is scary: In a recent national survey, 57 per cent said that, when an ingredient (like fat) was not listed on the package, that meant the ingredient wasn't there.

In the name of public health and disease prevention, the alliance wants easy-to-read listings on most foods. None of that should be too daunting for an industry that can tuck Mongolian fish genes into beets.

By itself, truth in packaging has a startling impact on what gets made and sold. The year after the U.S. began compulsory labelling, sales of high-fat ice cream went flat, and 1,500 reduced-fat products made their hasty debut.

The Council of Canadians, meanwhile, points out that every one of us is an unwitting subject in the mass testing of biotech foods.

Maybe GM foods will bring us enormous health benefits in the future. And maybe not.

Right now, the government is reviewing its labelling policies, and already the big food companies are lobbying against any change.

If you beg to disagree, write to Health Minister Allan Rock and tell him you want mandatory labelling of all nutritional ingredients. Be more like the English: Make a food fuss.

Toronto Star

"Good evening, we'd like to talk to you about genetically modified crops"

COMPREHENSION

1 How common is genetically engineered food? Give some examples.
2 What part of a scorpion might you find in your vegetables?
3 Why have British stores rejected GM foods?
4 Were 57% of Canadians right or wrong to think that an unlisted ingredient was not in a food product? Justify your answer with words from the text.
5 Why does the author think we should worry about GM foods?
6 Who does the author admire, and why?

 **AMMUNITION BOX**

Key words
technology *use of scientific or industrial methods*
crop *a plant that is sown by farmers, usually to be eaten*
yield *the amount of crops you get*
consequence *something that happens as a result of a particular action or set of conditions*
environment *the air, water and land in which people, animals and plants live*
to sow *to plant or scatter seeds*
test crops *crops that have been planted as a trial*
regulations *official rules*
consumer *someone who buys a product*

Handy hints
Agricultural production has dramatically increased, but at the expense of a number of food scares.

- Bovine Spongiform Encephalopathy (BSE or Mad Cow Disease) affected UK cattle in the 1990s. A fatal virus that attacks the brain, it is alleged to be connected to the human form (Creutzfeldt-Jakob disease) and led to a worldwide ban on British beef for some years. The disease was linked to cattle being given feed that was contaminated
- GM (genetically modified) food. This is food that has been altered by taking the genes from other species and adding them to a food to give it extra attributes (such as the beetle resistant potato in the article). Its supporters claim it will vastly improve agricultural yields, whilst its opponents claim it is untested and potentially dangerous
- EU law requires food ingredients containing GM soya or maize to be labelled, but where GM material – protein or DNA – is removed in the processing, the labels do not have to state that ingredients come from a GM source
- GM crops could help combat malnutrition, which affects about 800 million people, and feed the projected three billion growth in world population by 2030

ACTIVITIES

A Role-play: In groups of three. A firm producing GM foods has applied to the government for a licence to grow its products in your country. You have to make a decision on whether to grant the licence.

Student A, take the role of the minister:

- If you agree to grant the licence, the company will bring millions of pounds of investments into the country, which in turn will mean many new jobs. However, public opinion is currently anti GM foods and the move will prove very unpopular.
- If you don't agree, your decision will probably be popular with many people. However, the company will take its business to another country, and you will lose the investment, jobs, and knowledge in a new and potentially very lucrative technology.

Student B, take the role of the firm:

- You are keen to be granted this licence. You need to put forward the advantages of GM crops.

Student C, take the role of the farmer:

- You are keen for the experiment to go ahead, but want to know of any potential risks. Also, you are concerned about local reaction.

Make your decision using the information above and based on the group's feelings about GM foods. When you finish, compare your decision with those of other groups in the class. Were they the same, or very different?

B ✍ Imagine you live in Canada and read the article opposite. Write a letter to Health Minister Allan Rock and tell him your views on the subject of food labelling and GM foods.

Or

✍ Write an essay: GM foods will not combat world poverty. Discuss.

 **DISCUSSION**

1 Do you think food labelling is important? Why, why not?
2 Have there been any food scares in your country similar to the one in the UK (see ammunition box)? Describe them in detail.
3 Why do you think governments have been slow to enforce food labelling?
4 Do people have enough knowledge to make decisions about food matters, or should we leave them to government experts?
5 Who has more power in your country – the farmers, or the shops that sell the food?
6 How much do you personally care about what you eat? Do you follow a diet? Eat any special foods? Check food labels? Why, why not?
7 What's your opinion on GM foods (see ammunition box)?

 **NETWORKING**

Find out more about food technology.

Books: *Food Technology* by Jill Robinson
GM Free: Shopper's Guide to Genetically Modified Foods by Sue Dibb and Tim Lobstein
Genetic Engineering, Food, And Our Environment: A Brief Guide by Luke Anderson

Websites:
www.foe.co.uk
www.icta.org
www.monsanto.vigil.net/
www.purefood.org

- What do you know about the World Trade Organisation?
- Why do you think a world trade organisation is necessary?

The hidden tentacles of the world's most secret body

BY GEOFFREY LEAN
Environment correspondent

Tobacco pickers, Philippines

Behind the imposing entrance of a grand 1920s building on the shores of Lake Geneva lies what is probably the most powerful organisation on Earth. Far more potent than any government, its decisions are already affecting our lives and unleashing international conflicts. It can stop us choosing what we eat. It can strike down laws passed by even the strongest democratic governments. It can start or sanction trade wars and it can set at naught the provisions of international treaties which have been solemnly ratified by the world's nations.

The building belongs to the World Trade Organisation (WTO). This organisation, which sets the rules that govern how nations trade with each other, is about to become the centre of a gigantic battle for public opinion. This autumn it will begin a push, backed by many of the richest nations, to extend its powers even more. And some 700 organisations from 73 countries have sworn to stop it. These include Oxfam, Friends of the Earth and the Japanese Consumers' Union to small grassroots networks in the Third World. They have signed a joint declaration to 'oppose any effort to expand

the powers of the World Trade Organisation,' saying it has worked 'to prise open markets for the benefit of transnational corporations at the expense of national economies, workers, farmers and other people.'

Already the temperature is rising. Last week, the WTO ruled that the EU must drop an 11-year ban – imposed to safeguard health – on US beef treated with hormones. It authorised the Clinton administration to penalise European goods until it does.

It was never supposed to be like this. The WTO is the inheritor of a 50-year push to

promote free trade – a cause once as uncontroversial as freedom itself. However, the way it is using its powers is leading to a growing suspicion that its initials should really stand for World Take Over. In a series of rulings it has struck down measures to help the world's poor, protect the environment, and safeguard health in the interests of private – usually American – companies.

'The WTO seems to be on a crusade to increase private profit at the expense of all other considerations, including the well-being and quality of

life of the mass of the world's people,' says Ronnie Hall, trade campaigner at Friends of the Earth International. 'It seems to have a relentless drive to extend its power.'

Environmentalists and health campaigners fear that after slapping down such diverse 'impediments to free trade' as small Caribbean banana farmers, clean petrol, endangered turtles, and health precautions, it will now help the US government, Monsanto and other biotech companies make it impossible for people to refuse to eat genetically modified food.

Under new trade rules, the Philippines is importing American corn that is far cheaper than its local equivalent. As a result, says Oxfam, half a million poor Filipino farmers risk losing their livelihoods. And, it adds, the subsidy to each American farmer, at $29,000 (£17,000) a year, is 100 times higher than the average Filipino growers' entire average income. Aren't such subsidies an impediment to free trade? The WTO seems to have a selective view. While Third World countries are forbidden to subsidise their crops, Western nations quintupled their agricultural subsidies from $47 bn to $247 bn in the first four years of the WTO's existence.

Independent on Sunday

COMPREHENSION

1 Where is the WTO based?
2 What rules does the WTO set?
3 Why do certain groups such as Oxfam want to limit the powers of the WTO?
4 Name two issues that the WTO has made rulings on.
5 How have the WTO's rulings affected Philippine farmers?

AMMUNITION BOX

Key words

tariff *a charge made on incoming products*

free trade *where there are no tariffs*

protectionism *where a country uses tariffs to protect its industries/products*

duty *the tax paid on incoming goods*

imports *goods brought into a country*

exports *goods going abroad*

quota *a set number of goods – can be used as a maximum or minimum*

subsidy *a sum of money given by a government to help industry compete*

Handy hints

An impartial WTO ...?

- The WTO was formed in 1994 as a successor to Gatt (General Agreement on Trade and Tariffs) to promote free trade
- For more than 20 years the EU has helped small West Indian banana growers by favouring imports of their fruit. Three years ago the Clinton administration complained to the WTO that the EU scheme was unfair – even though the US has never exported a single banana. The complaint closely followed a $500,000 donation from Chiquita (a company that produces bananas) to the Democratic Party. The WTO upheld the complaint, and ordered the EU to stop its help
- Meanwhile, such long-term staple products as basmathi rice were able to be 'patented' by one US company. Since the WTO's existence, the share of world trade of the poorer countries has decreased

ACTIVITIES

A Role-play: In groups imagine you represent a group of West Indian banana growers who are finding it increasingly difficult to make a living. You have been asked to prepare a campaign to promote fairer world trade and stop large Western companies from undercutting you. You have to decide on the following:

- Your slogan
- Your aims
- Who you will petition
- How you will run your campaign (newspaper, TV, demonstrations)

Compare your ideas with those of other groups. Vote on who has the most effective campaign.

B ✍ Using the ideas from the speaking activity, write down the points you came up with in order to convince the WTO that things must change.

Harvesting wheat, USA

DISCUSSION

1 Whose interests do you think the World Trade Organisation serves?

2 Do you think the World Trade Organisation is necessary? Why, why not? How might the world be different if the World Trade Organisation didn't exist?

3 What do you think could be done to aid poorer countries?

4 Do you think rich countries have any obligation to help poorer countries? If so, how can they be forced to carry out these obligations?

5 Can Third World countries help themselves and each other in their dealings with the World Trade Organisation?

6 In countries such as America, businesses give money to political parties (see ammunition box). Do you think this should be either banned or controlled? Why, why not?

7 Look at the two photographs. What do they tell you about the countries?

8 How could the public alter the way the WTO works?

NETWORKING

Find out about other powerful world organisations.

Books: *International Economic Organisations and the Third World* by Marc Williams
The Times Guide to World Organisations: Their Role & Reach in the New World Order by Richard Owen

Film: *Enemy Of The State* (1998) directed by Tony Scott
The Pelican Brief (1993) directed by Joel Schumacher

Websites:
www.psa.as.uk/
www.nd.edu/~rop/

 **FOCUS**

● Who is the leader of your country? How visible is he/she to the public?

Today's Leaders live in cocoon of privilege

By Carol Goar

> *Politicians also have no leisure, because they are always aiming at ... power and glory, or happiness.*
>
> Aristotle 384–322 BC

HIS DISGUISE was amateurish. But the people didn't care. They were too delighted to discover King Abdullah posing as a television reporter in the Jordanian capital of Amman.

It would be nice if Prime Minister Jean Chrétien tried something like that. My political friends roll their eyes when I make such outlandish suggestions. A few, thinking I might be serious, point out no Western leader would take such a security risk or behave in such an undignified way.

Such objections are easily answered. Surely Canada is no more dangerous than Jordan.

And surely a royal heir educated at Britain's Royal Military Academy at Sandhurst, and Oxford University knows a bit about decorum.

In truth, I find the idea of Chrétien in dark glassess and a false moustache ludicrous.

But I do think some way has to be found to get political leaders out of their privileged cocoons. It troubles me that those we elect rapidly become isolated from the concerns of ordinary Canadians.

Chrétien, the self-styled 'little guy from Shawinigan,' has two official residences and a lakeside family retreat. He has a limousine to whisk him past poor neighbourhoods and a retinue of Mounties to keep strangers at a distance.

Ontario Premier Mike Harris, who calls himself one of 'the little people,' reacts with angry disbelief when his political opponents accuse him of hurting the poor.

He thinks slashing welfare benefits gives single mothers an incentive to work. He thinks low-income families should be grateful for tax cuts.

Both leaders have gone though painful personal ordeals while in office; Chrétien's adopted son was convicted of sexual assault and Harris separated from his wife.

But they remain far removed from the daily struggles of the average citizen. They have no idea how it feels to miss a rent payment or comb through the Help Wanted ads.

Many commentators would argue that it is impossible in today's world for a political leader to get out among the people.

I remain unconvinced.

Aspiring prime ministers and premiers seem to have no trouble doing it at election-time.

Nor do I accept that life at the top is so

rigidly structured that a leader can't control his or her own agenda. Chrétien finds time for four golf games a week. So why can't heads of government break out of their comfortable bubble?

It's partly a question of will.

Any social agency or charity would be happy to introduce Chrétien or Harris to its clients. But they prefer to speak to safe, partisan audiences.

It's also a question of political tactics.

One-to-one conversations with ordinary Canadians aren't a very efficient way to gain votes. Television advertising sways more people.

Listening to people's concerns isn't a very efficient way to sample public opinion. Polls are quicker and tidier.

The third factor is public expectations. If people say nothing when Harris vilifies teachers, nurses, welfare recipients and the church, he'll assume Ontarians approve of such tactics.

Apparently our politicians have gotten the message that we are satisfied with armchair leadership.

In Arab cultures, rulers are expected to leave their palaces every so often, and share the struggles and frustrations of their people.

We shouldn't need such traditions in a modern democracy. But we do.

Toronto Star

 **COMPREHENSION**

1. Which king disguised himself?
2. In your own words, describe how Chrétien and Harris like to appear to the public.
3. What is the main problem facing Chrétien and Harris?
4. What is the irony of leaders appearing in public?
5. How does the writer explain the reluctance of political leaders to mix with the public (give all the reasons)?
6. What does the writer say we can learn from the Arabs?

 **DISCUSSION**

1 Do you think King Abdullah's secret trips to meet his subjects are a good idea? Why, why not?

2 What reputation do politicians have in your country?

3 Do you think prime ministers and presidents need to remain isolated for their own security?

4 Why do you think people become politicians?

5 Do you think some leaders are over protected, and therefore lose touch with their country?

President Netanyahu and his family, surrounded by bodyguards.

ACTIVITIES

A Work in groups: there must be at least three groups in the class.

Imagine you are members of a new political party. The people have become disenchanted with other politicians, seeing them as out of touch and uncaring. Draw up a manifesto for your party. Explain how you are different, how you will improve politics, what your policies are, and why people should vote for you. Then elect a spokesperson to make a speech. When each group has spoken, elect a party.

B ✍ From the speaking activity, write up your party's manifesto. Feel free to use any of the other ideas you heard. Take care with your style – remember, you want to get people to vote for you!

 **NETWORKING**

Find out about politicians in your country. Are they isolated from the public, or involved in the everyday life of the country?

Books: *Diaries* by Alan Clark
Dutch: A Memoir of Ronald Reagan by Edmund Morris
Nelson Mandela by Jayne Woodhouse
The Downing Street Years by Margaret Thatcher

Films: *Absolute Power* (1997) directed by Clint Eastwood
Dave (1993) directed by Ivan Reitman
Wag the Dog (1997) directed by Barry Levinson

TV: *Yes, Minister*
Yes, Prime Minister

Websites:
www.parliament.uk/
www.whitehouse.gov/

AMMUNITION BOX

Key words
manifesto *a document explaining a political party's objectives*
policy *a plan of action*

Handy hints
• **Democracy**
The word comes from two Greek words, *demos* – people, and *kratis* – rule
• **Suffrage**
Suffrage is the right to vote. It has often been withheld on grounds of race, prosperity (only those with money could vote) or gender. Only in 1893, in New Zealand were women allowed to vote. It took until 1971 in Switzerland. But it has been a struggle for the majority of men, too. In the United States, when the Constitution was first published 200 years ago, it has been estimated only 6% of men were eligible to vote
• **Money**
Running a democracy can be expensive. In the '96 presidential election it took $10 million to put a Republican into the White House ... and that was the 1896 election! One modern-day senator, Russ Feingold, has described the process as 'legalised bribery'
• **Voting**
Some countries have fought hard to achieve the vote. But those who have it do not always exercise it. In the UK, in 1999, barely a quarter of the population bothered to vote in the European elections. Various solutions have been proposed such as allowing people to vote in supermarkets, on the Internet, or passing laws forcing people to vote

Hidden politicians

- At what age do most people leave home in your country?
- Do some adults continue to live at home with their parents?

Homeboys

Simon Brooke

I used to laugh at my mate Ted. Why? Ted is 32 and still lives at home. A surveyor, he earns a good salary, has a girlfriend and lots of mates but he still lives with his parents.

The image of the grown man treated like a kid by his bossy, overbearing mother is always good for a laugh. So, we used to laugh at Ted. I say we used to laugh because soon afterwards it dawned on me there are advantages to living at home. 'Dad pays the bills, Mum does my washing and cooks my dinner,' he says. Ted is part of a growing trend. In nearly one in ten British homes, the children are independent adults. More than half of all young men aged 24 now live at home compared with just 48% in 1979. A quarter of men in their late twenties live with their parents compared to less than a fifth twenty years ago. Even among 30-34 year-olds the figure has increased from one in 11 to one in nine.

Needless to say economics have a lot to do with this. The average age of first time buyers has risen from 27 to 32 in the past decade.

'I don't think people in the nineties are as keen to buy their own flats,' says twenty-nine year-old Mark who lives with his parents. 'I enjoyed sharing a flat so I've proved I can do it but I don't feel the need to get my own place yet. Besides I help my Mum and Dad around the house.'

This last comment brings a snort of indignant laughter from Mark's sister who moved out when she was 18. 'Shopping, cooking and housework are still considered women's work,

especially by our parents' generation. Mum and I would fall out in no time over what to cook. Mark hasn't got a clue and my parents wouldn't expect him to. She may complain, but Mum loves still feeding him and doing his ironing.'

Changing attitudes towards masculinity are also partly responsible believes Mick Cooper, a lecturer in counselling at Brighton University. 'Men don't feel that living at home detracts from their masculinity.'

Recently a woman in Italy got so fed up with looking after her forty year-old son that she changed the locks of the family home. He took her to court where the judge decided he could move back in immediately because a parent's obligation to provide support should go on either until the child has had enough or the parent died. But despite this now notorious ruling, in Italy the situation is in reverse according to Emilia Fantzoni, an Italian journalist living in London. 'Even ten years ago for a man and a woman to live together without being married was the cause of gossip. Now it is quite acceptable, especially in the big cities. It's causing a lot of anguish amongst traditional Italian mothers.' Ted sympathises. 'Let's face it, most mothers would like their sons to stay at home if they could. In many ways I'm just doing it to keep my Mum happy.'

You're an angel, Ted.

Midweek

COMPREHENSION

1 How old is Ted?
2 What are the benefits of living at home for Ted?
3 How might Mark's mother treat Mark and his sister differently?
4 What does Mark's sister think about him living at home?
5 How did the Italian judge see the responsibilities of parents to their children?
6 What reason does Ted give for living at home?

ACTIVITIES

A Role-play: Son/daughter: You are an only child aged 25, with a good job. You live at home rent-free. Your salary is spent on your social life, travel and your car. Your parents, who are retired, have no financial problems and you don't pay them rent. As for housework, you are at work all day and your parents are at home, so they see to the household chores. You are happy to live at home, but recently your parents have seemed grumpy towards you. Feel free to remind them of their responsibilities to you.

Mother/father: Your son/daughter has a well-paid job, and you would like them to continue to live at your home. However, they don't pay rent and expect you to do all the housework. Recently you have been unwell and get tired very easily. At 65 you are finding running the family too much. You want to try and work out a fair agreement if your son/daughter is to stay at home.

B ✍ Write an essay: Leaving home is a vital part of growing up.

Or

✍ Write a letter to Ted. Tell him what you think of his ideas of still living at home while in his thirties.

DISCUSSION

1 What are the pros and cons of adults living with their parents?
2 Who normally leaves home first in your country, sons or daughters?
3 If you have already left home, why did you leave (marriage, a job, another reason)? Would you ever move back?
4 If you are still living at home, do you plan to leave? Are you staying for purely financial reasons?
5 Should parents have the right to force their children to leave home? If so, under what circumstances? Or do children have the right to insist on staying in the family home as long as they wish?
6 Do you think that adults living with their parents and not buying property could affect the economy of a country? Why would this be?
7 Do you think parents should also be able to live in their grown-up children's homes? Why, why not?
8 Do you think children should be forced to leave home at a certain age? Why, why not?

AMMUNITION BOX

Key words
nuclear family *seen as the 'traditional' family of Mum, Dad and two/three children*
extended family *this type of family is increasing. It can include a married couple who have children from previous marriages*
mortgage *an agreement under which a bank or building society lends a person money to buy a property*
lifestyle *how a person lives his/her life*
responsibilities *having certain duties*
rent *regular payment made for accommodation*

Should I stay or should I go?

Reasons to stay	Reasons to go
No mortgage or rent	A chance for independence
Someone else to do the chores	Opportunity to live by your own rules
Someone else to pay the bills	Financial independence from parents

NETWORKING

Find out more about men and women who can't leave home.

Book: *Absent Fathers, Lost Sons* by Guy Corneau

TV: *Mrs Merton*

Website:
www.the menscenter.com/

- Do you think it is important to be able to express yourself in your own language?
- Do you think some languages are dying out?

Silent witnesses

Hugh Brody charts the repressive effects of colonialism on human expression

Human beings make about 160 different sounds. This is the sum of the vocal elements of all the world's languages. English, one of the more complicated vocal systems, has about 55 of these sounds. Norwegian has 75. The Bushman or San languages of the Kalahari have more than 145. The San are the great acrobats of the mouth. In their campaigns against tribes, the colonists have despised them for the very sounds of their voices and have sought to eradicate their languages.

Throughout the world, there has been a drastic loss of tribal languages. Some linguists estimate that some 5,000 languages or distinctive dialects have faded away this century. The loss of these ways of speaking and of knowing is a loss of genius that may well be irrecoverable. It is also a cause of intense grief and disorientation to hundreds of thousands of tribal people, who struggle to be themselves without the words to say what that means.

In southern Africa, Dutch settlers dismissed the KhoiSan ways of speaking as 'gibberings of monkeys'. In both the US and Canada, those concerned to deal with 'the Indian problem' in the nineteenth century resolved that 'those barbaric tongues' would be eradicated, making way for the English that 'all who are civilised can understand'.

The Europeans' assault on tribal languages is well documented, and most persistent when its victims have been hunter-gatherers. These were the tribes whose ways of life meant they were spread far and wide across settlement frontiers. There seems to have been a compulsion to achieve, in these places, a final and decisive silence.

Their barbaric tongues would cease, to be replaced by English, Spanish, Portuguese, French, Afrikaans – any language of 'civilisation'.

Tribal people often say that to have stories about a land is to own it. The stories that hold the knowledge and sustain the links with the spirits are a permanent challenge, a rival to the territory. No wonder, then, that the surviving descendants of these tribes have an intensely difficult and complicated relationship to their own voices. They often speak the languages of their oppressors and have absorbed the lessons of their oppressors: indigenous customs, history and ways of speech are matters of shame. Many tribal peoples have survived by remaining silent and unnoticed, at the margins of the colonial world.

Yet the silence, in many parts of the world, is being broken. With land claim movements, cultural revival, anti-colonial protest, a refusal to disappear. Tribal voices are making themselves heard. There are assertions of pride and rights: to know their place is to claim it, whatever the colonialists might say.

In Australia, Aboriginal groups are defending every part that remains of their heritage and lands. For tribal people, the connections between language and land are self-evident. From the point of view of settlers and their nation states, these are marginal, infertile territories. They are the lands where tribal people have been able to endure. They are languages that somehow 'belong to the past'. Modern tribes are not arguing for a reinstatement of the past. Rather, they seek to have their own resources with which to prosper in the present. With the lands and languages that are theirs, their lives can be full of opportunity and the strength of cultural and individual health.

The Guardian

Sahara bushman

> The loss of a language is part of the more general loss being suffered by the world, the loss of diversity in all things.
>
> Ken Hale, linguist

COMPREHENSION

1 How many sounds can humans make?
2 How many dialects were lost in the 20th century?
3 What languages replaced the dialects?
4 Are tribes beginning to make themselves heard?
5 What do modern tribes need to prosper?

AMMUNITION BOX

Key words
ethnic *a race or group that has a common cultural tradition*
culture *ideas and beliefs that are shared by people in a society*
heritage *customs and traditions that have been in a society for a long time*
roots *a connection with the place where you were born*
ancestor *a member of your family who lived a long time ago*
moribund *dying out*
extinction *when something (a plant, animal or language) no longer exists*
to die out *to disappear, no longer exist*

Handy hints
- 150 North American Indian languages, about 80% of the existing ones, are not spoken
- There are 40 dead languages in Alaska and northern Siberia, 160 in Central and South America, 45 in Russia, perhaps 3,000 worldwide
- Between 3,600 and 5,400 languages, as many as 90% of the world's total, are threatened with extinction in the 21st century

Source: *The Language Instinct* by Steven Pinker

ACTIVITIES

A Role-play: In groups of five. John Stevens is 14 years old and a pupil at a high school in America. Although of American Indian origin, he was adopted by white parents at birth. His parents are keen that he studies his native language and culture, and the school supports them in this. However, John sees these lessons as a waste of time and would rather study Spanish as it's more useful.
His parents and the school think he is wasting a valuable opportunity, and will regret it when he's older. Students A, B and C should present their case to the school governors (D and E) who will make a decision.

> **Student A,** play the part of John. Explain why you want to learn Spanish and your reasons for not studying more about native American history. Invent any details you need

> **Students B and C,** play John's adoptive parents. You feel it is important he maintains some contact with his past. You are worried that when John is older he might blame you for his lack of knowledge about his heritage. He can study Spanish at any time – but this is a valuable opportunity. Invent any details you need

> **Students D and E,** play the part of two school governors. You need to listen to both sides of the argument and make a decision. Be prepared to justify your decision

Each group then compares its final decision with those of other groups in the class.

B Write an essay: The loss of language is not something to be regretted. Rather, the sooner the world only speaks one language the better.

DISCUSSION

1 Do you think it is important to maintain tribal languages? Why, why not?

2 Would it be a bad thing if the world only spoke three or four languages? Why, why not?

3 How important is a language to national identity?

4 Do you think having many languages in one country can create problems?

5 Do you see English as a threat to your language? Why, why not?

6 What other reasons are there for languages dying out?

7 How can tribal languages be protected?

NETWORKING

Find out about any dialects spoken in your country.

Books: *Hold Your Tongue: Bilingualism and the Politics of English Only* by James Crawford
Mother Tongue by Bill Bryson
The Language Instinct by Steven Pinker

Film: *Nell* (1994) directed by Michael Apted

Play: *Mountain Language* by Harold Pinter

Websites:
Ourworld.compuserve.com

31

- How important is money to you personally?
- Do you see money as fundamentally good or evil?

No need to apologise for BMWs or blondes

Mary Ellen Synon

MAKING money solves most problems, and in Ireland today, plenty of men are making plenty of money. The only reasonable response is a cry of, 'Well done.' Yet instead we are hearing complaints that too many Irish are now making too much money. We are hearing accusations of greed, and criticism about pressure. Why?

Because there are people who are envious, mean-spirited, and incapable. And when they see other people enchanted with making money, they can only hiss and begrudge. One could say their complaints are pettiness and ought to be ignored.

But I believe it is more than just begrudgery. And I believe there is danger. For, although there is no more virtuous activity than making money, even the Irishmen who do it best do not seem to understand why it is such a good thing.

Certainly they know that making money makes their life better. But they have no understanding of the morality of what they are doing. You can hear their uncertainty when they talk about their work. An industrialist says he has been 'lucky' and points to how many jobs his industry has created: but wealth is never built by luck, it is built by brains. And the point of industry is profit.

You know a man understands the morality of money when he says, 'I had the idea for this factory. I took the risk, put in the long hours to make it work. And every year, I intend to get more productivity out of every worker, and deliver more profit to myself. And I love it.'

Yes, of course such a man will create employment, will have a healthy effect on local life. But none of this is the point. He is making money through trade: that is virtuous.

Trade is the means by which man gets what he wants, freely and without coercion. It is the free exercise of an individual's judgement in pursuit of whatever he values.

What the begrudgers say is, 'He has plenty' never 'earns plenty' as though the wealth just existed by chance 'so we must redistribute it.' That is greed. And the danger of the capitalists' ignorance of their virtue lies just there: they do not understand that to capitulate to redistribution is wrong.

A man's money is a man's liberty.

When the State controls a man's money, it controls the man. That is why the liberty of citizens rests in many people having lots of money. When private citizens have money, they must use it wisely, or lose it to more clever citizens, in whose hands the stuff will be better used.

When the State has money, it is used for political purposes. Money in their hands produces nothing. In private hands, it produces goods, services, jobs, decent houses, healthy teeth, well-educated children, safer cars, and all the other things that make life agreeable.

It also produces, around the fringes, blondes, Armani suits, and Rolex watches. And while those may be irritating, they are never compulsory.

The meat and potatoes are work, productivity, creativity, investment, and profit, Irishmen shaping their lives through their own work with their own money. Why begrudge them a blonde and a Hermes tie?

COMPREHENSION

1 Are people who make money praised for it?
2 What is the ultimate aim of business?
3 Explain in your own words how the writer sees trade?
4 Why is money better in private hands?
5 Why should we not begrudge the rich their little luxuries?

"Out here a guy could be lulled into thinking that there is more to life than just power or money."

DISCUSSION

1 How important is money in your society? What else does your society value?

2 Do you agree with the way the writer sees trade? What kinds of 'coercion' might there be in reality?

3 Can you think of any activity 'more virtuous' than making money? If so, what is it, and why is it more virtuous?

4 Is money ever better used in public hands rather than private hands?

5 Does having money improve life for individuals?

6 Does having money generally have a positive or negative effect on people's character? Justify your answer.

ACTIVITIES

A Imagine you've been given £100,000 to spend in one week. Working in groups, decide how you're going to use it. What are you going to buy? Are you going to make any investments? Will you give any to family/friends/charity? Come to a group decision, then compare your ideas with those of other groups in the class. Did you find your plans were very similar or quite different? What do you think your plans say about your character?

B ✍ Write a letter to the newspaper that printed the article, giving your own personal views.

Or

✍ Write an essay: How a million changed my life!

AMMUNITION BOX

Key words
investment *the money put into an account or company in order to make a profit*
capital *money or property*
account *where money is held at a bank*
funds *money available*
money market *banks and other institutions that buy, lend or borrow money for profit*
financial *to do with money*
affluence *wealth*
prosperous *successful*

Handy hints
- Ancient coins were probably first invented in China, and appeared again in what is now modern-day Turkey in c 700BC
- Paper money was also invented in China, while banks and credit existed in Ancient Babylon (now part of Iraq), Greece and Rome, all well over 2000 years ago!
- The birth of modern capitalist thought is often ascribed to the book *Wealth of Nations* by Adam Smith, 1776. He preached that economic freedom ("laissez-faire") with as little government control as possible was the best way for countries to enrich themselves
- The opposite of this was Karl Marx's *Das Kapital* (*Capital*), 1867, which argued capitalism meant the concentration of wealth in the hands of a few rich, and that they would then be overthrown by revolution and a system of communism – central economic control by a government to achieve a fairer balance

NETWORKING

Find out about financial institutions around the world.

Books: *Bonfire of the Vanities* by Tom Wolfe
A Christmas Carol by Charles Dickens
The Money Drunk by Mark Bryan and Julia Cameron

Films: *Wall Street* (1987) directed by Oliver Stone
Trading Places (1983) directed by John Landis

Play: *Money* by Carol Churchill

Websites:
www.bundesbank.de
www.stw.org/
www.worldbank.org/

- Do men and women in your country have very defined roles? For example, do the men provide for the women, while the women look after the children and the house?
- How do you think these roles have evolved, how are they changing today?

MEN FORCED TO BE WIVES

Denise Dowling reports

In an unusual festival in northern Greece, husbands and wives swap roles for one day

Nikos Mitrelis's list of chores is long: sweep steps, hang laundry, scrub bathroom, get groceries, cook soup. His wife Dina, meanwhile, reclines on a sofa. Dressed in his wife's bathrobe, apron and headscarf, Nikos fetches her a coffee. Dina sips it and scans the morning paper. He parts the lace curtains and peers outside. Thankfully, no one has witnessed his servile behaviour.

But despite appearances, Nikos is not that rarity in Greece – a subservient husband. He may be henpecked this morning, but he rules the roost during the rest of the year. For today is *Gynaikratia* (women in charge), a role-reversal festival held on 8th January each year in several villages of north-eastern Greece.

During *Gynaikratia*, men are forbidden to leave their home. If one is imprudent enough to venture outdoors, the women have been known to beat him.

While some of the women take it easy, others are taking care of business – like the two dressed as police officers. In a blue uniform and white high heels, Teresa blows a whistle to stop traffic. 'Today this village is honouring the rule of women. Would you like to donate money to the women's union?' The money will pay for the women to take a holiday, leaving their husbands at home.

By now, some men have taken the risk of breaking their curfew and wander by, sulkily swinging worry beads. A hunched man hobbles past, raising his cane like an exclamation mark. 'Women should not have rights for the day,' he says. 'Not even for an hour.'

Janios Theofilikieas and his cronies admit to being domestically challenged on the other 364 days of the year. 'It's a matter of pride,' the farmer explains. 'The older men believe it's a woman's job to do the housework and care for the children.'

'Last year my husband dressed as a woman and did the housework,' says Janios's wife Julia. 'But his friends teased him so much, he refused to do it this year.' Their fifteen-year-old daughter Niki shudders as she recalls the meals her father served.

Dimos Somalos, 69, is feeding his grandchild. He delicately spoons in strained carrots while Marina covers her mouth to hide the giggles. 'It's better that women care for babies and the house,' she says, 'because men don't know what they're doing.'

Dimos seems to be enjoying himself, bustling about with baby food and hanging laundry. But he says there is one task he won't perform. 'I don't change nappies,' he laughs. 'That is not a man's job.' The couple's son, however, is quite open about helping his wife at home. 'But they live in Athens, so it's different,' Dimos says.

Then they travel to the local hall where only women are admitted. Inside they drink from bottles of retsina, but even though the conversation grows increasingly raucous with every swig, the women remain fairly decorous. However, they have been known, later in the evening, to imitate their men by stuffing potatoes in their pants and chasing each other around the room.

'When I marry, I want my husband to help me with the housework,' Niki announces. 'I want to marry, though it is also good to be single.' Her cousin Aleka smiles with a wisdom greater than her nineteen years and says, 'But if a woman is not married, she is free.'

Marie Claire

COMPREHENSION

1 What happens in the festival?
2 Who is normally in charge in Nikos' household?
3 What will the women do with the money they collect?
4 How good does Janios Theofilikieas think he and his friends are at doing the housework?
5 Which member of Dimos' family is happy to do his share of the housework? Why?
6 What does the writer mean by, 'with a wisdom greater than her 19 years'?

 **AMMUNITION BOX**

Key words

male chauvinism *prejudiced attitude of certain men who believe they are superior to women*

feminism *belief in the principle that women should have the same rights and opportunities as men*

stereotype *an image, idea or character that has become fixed or standardised in a conventional form without individuality*

Handy hints

- The Equal Opportunities Commission (EOC) is the expert body on equality between men and women in the UK. It was created by Parliament in 1976 to try to end sex discrimination and promote equal opportunities between men and women
- Women still earn less than men in the UK. Women in their twenties earn 92% of the male wage, while the average gross weekly pay is 72.5% of men's earnings
- Employed fathers work an average of 20 hours a week more than employed mothers. The working week of fathers is four hours longer than men without children

DISCUSSION

1 How would your society react to the idea of forcing husbands to be housewives for one day each year?

2 Do you think that some women would prefer to stay at home and look after their children while their partners supported them? Give your reasons.

3 Do you think women should receive some kind of payment for looking after the home?

4 In your country, are there some men who stay at home while the woman goes out to work? How are these men viewed? Do you think it is a good idea?

5 Are there some jobs in your country that are still dominated by men? If so, which jobs and why?

ACTIVITIES

A Work in groups of four or five.

You have been commissioned by your local government to come up with ideas for organising a festival in your town similar to the one in Greece. However,

- Some men have complained about the festival, saying it shouldn't go ahead. They believe the festival is an insult to them, disrupts their lives, and that what happens in the home is private
- The women are strongly in favour of the festival, saying it's only a bit of fun, it's their one day off, and it helps their men realise what life is like for them. If it is banned, say the women, then something should be done either to make men help at home, or to pay women for their work

Make your recommendations, and be prepared to justify them! You will have to try and please both the men and women! If there is more than one group in the class, compare your ideas.

B Write an essay: Men and women will never be equal, they are too different. Discuss.

 **NETWORKING**

Find out how women's roles have changed in your country in the past 30 years. How have men been affected by these changes?

Books: *Men Are From Mars, Women Are From Venus* by John Gray
Raising Boys by Steve Biddulph
Stiffed by Susan Faludi
The Ax by Donald Westlake
Why Men Don't Iron: The Real Science of Gender Studies by Anne and Bill Moir
Why Sex Is Fun by Jared Diamond

Films: *American Beauty* (1999) directed by Sam Mendes
The Fight Club (1999) directed by David Fincher

Websites:
www.eoc.org.uk
www.women.com/

- Why do people get married? Think of as many reasons as you can.
- Describe a typical wedding ceremony in your country.

A Slight Hitch

Philip Carey *marries a stranger*

It's no coincidence that weddings only come at the end of novels and films. The message is clear. Get married: The End.

After three years in LA, I'd pretty much become immune to the average Los Angelino. But when a 24-year-old Californian let herself into my apartment, it was worthy of a raised eyebrow. 'Hi, I'm CJ, I met your roommate. He said you needed to get married to stay in the country. I'll marry you.'

It was that simple. I was only a couple of weeks away from Immigration running me out of the US, but marriage? To an obviously mad stranger? I looked her up and down. She had a flat stomach, and most of her own teeth. I accepted.

The true gravity of the situation started to become apparent when my fiancé's mother called up to confirm the chapel. Apparently CJ's family would be attending. This was no longer the carefree affair I had imagined. What was I doing?

It was 11am, three hours till showdown. I woke up to a pounding on the hotel-room door. CJ was asleep. The less I remembered about this, the better. My best man was at the door to remind me I hadn't bought the rings, so we headed off to the mall. Fortuitously, this was located next to a bar. Having enjoyed 'one last swifty' three or four times, we were left with ten minutes to buy the rings, grab a taxi to the hotel, get changed and meet the limo.

I hit the hotel room at a sprint, two $20 rings in my pocket. CJ was still asleep. Not only were we horribly late but she still had to buy new shoes.

I called the chapel. My panic was unfounded. Yes, I could reschedule. What about 4.20 or 4.35 or 4.50? I breathed a sigh of relief.

Then CJ tapped me on the shoulder. 'You do love me, don't you?' I hardly knew this person. I nodded and retreated to the hotel bar. By the time we were cruising along the strip, the 'I love yous' were flowing freely. I loved CJ, I loved marriage, I even loved the squat, bearded limousine driver.

The first stop was City Hall for a marriage licence. We each took a form – requiring just name, address, date and place of birth, intended spouse. The laxity regarding identification also came as a surprise. All you need is a birth certificate. No passport, no photo ID.

Next stop, the chapel. There was the family to meet: plus hordes of well-meaning people from places I'd never heard of.

CJ sprinted up the aisle, dragging me with her. We stood at the altar. She rolled her eyes each time 'respect and honour' were mentioned, then giggled 'I will'.

And that was it. I smiled and posed for photos afterwards but couldn't shake the empty feeling inside. I just wanted my bed.

The black cloud of the night before lifted with the sun. Morning had arrived. I hadn't been drained of the will to live. Maybe I could do this. 'So,' CJ finally said. 'Tell me about yourself. What do you do?'

ARENA

COMPREHENSION

1 Where did the writer live?
2 How long had he lived there?
3 Why did the writer need to get married?
4 When did the writer first begin to worry about his coming marriage?
5 How strict were the official requirements for getting a licence? Give details.
6 How did the writer feel immediately after the ceremony? Why?

DISCUSSION

1 Do you think that the writer's marriage to CJ will last? Why, why not?

2 Do people take the idea of marriage seriously in your country?

3 Many people nowadays get married on tropical islands, in castles, even while doing a parachute jump. Do you think the wedding ceremony is important? If not, why not?

4 Do you think gay couples should also be able to get married? Why, why not?

5 In the UK, the number of couples getting married is falling. Is the same happening in your country? Why, why not?

6 Would you consider marrying a stranger if it was the only way to stay in a foreign country?

7 How acceptable is it for people to live together unmarried in your country? Has this affected the number of people getting married?

8 Would you like to get married or would you be happy to live with your partner? Why, why not?

ACTIVITIES

A In groups look at the list of qualities below. Select the five most important qualities you think necessary for marriage. Compare your group's list with others in the class and discuss any differences.

> *physical appearance   sense of humour   honesty   friendliness   generosity*
> *financial independence   age   parents' wishes   job   love   respect*
> *patience   health*

B Write an essay: Marriage has no place in society in the 21st century. Discuss

"SORRY I'M LATE. I HAD TO GET A TATTOO REMOVED."

NETWORKING

Find out more about marriage in your country.

Books: *Pride and Prejudice* by Jane Austen
Sense and Sensibility by Jane Austen

Film: *Four Weddings and a Funeral* (1994) directed by Mike Newell
Green Card (1990) directed by Peter Weir
Muriel's Wedding (1994) directed by P.J. Hogan
Runaway Bride (1999) directed by Gary Marshall
The Philadelphia Story (1940) by George Cukor
Very Bad Things (1998) directed by Peter Berg

Website:
www.marriagetools.com/

AMMUNITION BOX

Key words
marriage of convenience
getting married for a reason other than being in love (such as staying in a country)
arranged marriage
where your parents/family choose a partner for you
shotgun wedding
marrying because of pregnancy
a love match
marrying for love

Handy hints
- In 1996, there were 279,000 marriages in the UK compared to 348,000 in 1986
- Two in five marriages in the UK are expected to end in divorce
- The average age of bridegrooms is 33.6 years and of brides is 31.1 years
- Many people cohabit (live together without being married), but they are nine times more likely to split up than married couples
- One in three people say they get married to strengthen their relationship, while one in five marry because of their children
- By the late 1980s, 40% of people getting married had lived together first
- In 1960, almost 90% of American households with children under 18 were headed by married couples; by 1994, that figure had fallen to 75%

Sources: http://194.130.56.40/hi/english/uk/newsid_375000/375243.stm
http://www.topchoice.com/~psyche/pcthoh.html

- What do you know about space exploration?
- Would you like to travel in space?

Life support

Charles Duke is one of nine surviving astronauts who stood on the Moon. He and his wife Dorothy describe the highs and lows of being involved in the space programme

Charles Duke: I remember vividly the day I volunteered for the space programme. Dottie was very supportive. But my new job brought instant success and celebrity, and my ego swelled. Things were starting to go wrong between us, as I was so strongly focussed on my career. Being chosen for one of the later Apollo missions is still one of the high points of my life. Our view of the Earth was the most spectacular sight I'd ever seen, and I walked in wonder on the Moon. It was an incredibly still, crater-pocked, awesome environment.

Everyone knows about Buzz Aldrin's alcoholism, but I think all 12 of us who've been there were left with a heavy sense of, 'What now?' afterwards. I stayed to work on the Space Shuttle. It wasn't the same, the buzz was gone. Money became my goal, and I was working even longer hours than before.

It was a strange time, which Dorothy and I should have helped each other through, but we ended up competing. I was more of a military drill sergeant than a father, I was always demanding perfection. Things got much worse before I could learn to be more calm and encouraging. We had a different relationship after that.

I'm retired from the military now, but am active in business, and Dottie and I are involved in a Christian ministry. We're still not perfect, but we're best friends. I feel lucky that we found the strength to love and accept one another, because once you do that, you start to change.

Dorothy Duke: Test pilot school and the space programme never seemed that dangerous, because it was always very structured and controlled. Anyway, Charlie has always taken the typical pilot attitude of 'Oh, it'll never happen to me, I'm too smart.' But there was anxiety. The difficult thing was the constant separation, so it was almost a relief to finally get to Charlie's flight (Apollo 16).

I've never seen Charlie so excited as when he first came back. But then it was straight on to Apollo 17. I'd been hoping for a new beginning, more family time after the lunar landing, but it never came. It just seemed to get worse as Charlie struggled with the comedown. I cried a lot. Then I decided I was going to divorce him. The only thing to stop me was a nagging feeling that maybe this perfect husband I was looking for wasn't out there. The next logical step seemed to be suicide, and I thought about that. Once, I recall telling him about these thoughts, and he rolled over and went back to sleep!

The change came one day when some people visited our church. Like a lot of Americans, I'd always gone out of habit, despite being agnostic at best, but what they said about the power of prayer really moved me. I developed the ability to forgive Charlie. Finally, the change in me affected him and now we're very contented. The pain we went through was worthwhile. We've been part of each other's journey.

The Observer

1 Why is Charles Duke famous?
2 What was the Moon like?
3 What were the astronauts' feelings on being back on Earth?
4 How did space travel affect Charles Duke and his family?
5 How did Charles Duke behave towards his wife and family?
6 Why did things improve between him and his wife?

'I believe this nation should commit itself to achieving the goal, before this decade is out, of landing a man on the moon and returning him safely to Earth.'

President Kennedy

DISCUSSION

1 Why do you think man is so fascinated by space?

2 The Moon landings have been called the greatest achievement in history. Do you agree? Why, why not?

3 Do you think it is right to spend so much money on exploring space, when there are so many problems on Earth? Justify your answer.

4 What are the benefits of exploring space?

5 Do you think man will ever live on another planet? Why, why not?

6 Why do you think the astronauts found it so hard to get used to being back on Earth?

7 Do you think the novelty of space exploration has worn off, or are people still interested in new discoveries?

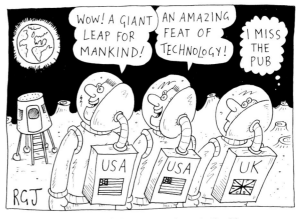

Why the British have never been to the Moon.

AMMUNITION BOX

Key words

launch *to send a spacecraft into space*

to orbit *to travel in a circle around the Earth or another planet*

cosmos *the universe*

shuttle *a spacecraft that can fly to space and return to Earth*

Handy hints

- The space race to the Moon began in 1957 with the launch of Sputnik 1 by the Soviet Union. This was followed by Sputnik 2 carrying a dog called Laika. Then Yuri Gagarin became the first person to go into space and orbit the Earth in 1961

- On May 25th 1961, President John F. Kennedy set America the challenge to land on the Moon by the end of the decade. America succeeded. Apollo 11 became the first manned mission to the Moon, landing on July 20th 1969

- The Apollo programme cost $25 billion and landed 12 men on the Moon between July 20th 1969 and 11th December 1972

- Apollo 1 caught fire during a preflight test and three astronauts were killed

- Apollo 13 had to abort its landing and return to Earth

NETWORKING

Find out more about space exploration. What other countries have been involved apart from America?

Books: *A Man on the Moon: The Voyages of the Apollo Astronauts* by Andrew L.Chaikin and Tom Hanks

The Right Stuff by Tom Wolfe

Films: *2001: A Space Odyssey* (1968) directed by Stanley Kubrick

Apollo 13 (1995) directed by Ron Howard

Star Wars (1977) directed by George Lucas

The Right Stuff (1983) directed by Philip Kaufman

Websites:
www.buzzaldrin.com/
www.doc.mmu.ac.uk/hst/photos-i.html
www.levc.nasa.gov
www.nasm.edu
www.nss.org

ACTIVITIES

A Role-play: In groups, imagine you are the team in charge of Project Mars, an internationally-manned expedition to Mars. The crew will be in space for 18 months and the expedition will be physically and mentally very demanding. It is up to you to choose the crew leader. You have drawn up the following shortlist:

Igor Yurev:
Russia's finest cosmonaut. He is extremely fit, experienced and very knowledgeable. However, his English is weak, and this may lead to problems in communication with the rest of the crew.

Mike Lehman:
German. Although an experienced astronaut, he has never led a mission before and on simulation exercises, he has panicked. However, he has the best knowledge of Mars out of all the candidates.

Sarah Simmons:
American. One of the first women to command a shuttle mission. Her work record is exemplary. However, the space programme has cost her her first marriage, and it seems her second is also in trouble.
Note: Her present husband has secretly written to the project asking that she not be chosen.

Harry Hammond:
American. Original choice as mission leader (Harry's father was part of the Apollo team). He is NASA's senior pilot and has successfully led seven missions, all with excellent results. However, last month he blacked out during training practice. Although the doctors can find nothing wrong with him, his health is a worry, as he may black out again.

Choose one of these people to be crew leader. Remember to justify your choice. Compare your choice with other groups in the class.

B Write up your recommendations to NASA in the form of a report. State why you rejected the other candidates, who your choice is, and why, in your opinion, that is the best choice.

 **FOCUS**

- Do you use the Internet? If yes, how do you use it?
- Do you think it would be possible to survive for 100 hours with no access to the outside world except through the Internet? What problems might you have?

My Internet hell

As an experiment, four volunteers each lived alone for 100 hours. They were dressed only in a bathrobe and had to get everything that they needed from the Internet

A dazed but relieved Emma Gibson told of her 'seedy' ordeal yesterday after four days trapped in cyberspace.

With three other volunteers, the out-of-work actress had agreed to be locked alone in a small room with just a computer and the Internet for company.

One hundred hours, three marriage proposals and dozens of lewd messages later, Miss Gibson, 30, emerged blinking into the sunshine rather glad the experience was over.

With the eyes of the world quite literally upon her – small cameras broadcast her every move on the Web – Internet Heaven had become more of a nightmare at times. 'I wanted to get out at the end. Too much Internet is bad for the health,' she said.

Net users were able to contact her using e mails or chat rooms – electronic conversation forums.

Miss Gibson, from London, added: 'Chat rooms are a pretty seedy experience in my view, especially if you are female and being viewed by a web-camera. It attracts a few perverts. I was being looked at and when someone was getting pervy with their language, a towel went over the camera.'

Miss Gibson was chosen from more than 250 applicants for the experiment. Shut up in a secure room at a central London hostel, she had to take off all her clothes and was given a bathrobe, a credit card and a budget of £500 to feed, clothe and amuse herself with all purchases ordered via the Internet. Organisers eventually had to start deleting all the abusive mail before it appeared on screen. Three men also offered proposals of marriage. 'I didn't accept any,' said Miss Gibson.

To keep sane during her confinement, Miss Gibson managed to download software from an Australian radio station to pipe out constant music. 'Spending time on your own in a room in front of a computer does change the way you see the world. My thought processes became quite obtuse. It was draining but I became quite addicted. I had to get out.'

She was going straight out for a stiff gin and tonic and a walk in the fresh air. 'I'm definitely not going on the Net for a few days.' Results of the experiment, organised by Microsoft, will be studied by Dr Helen Petrie, of the University of Hertfordshire.

Despite their reservations she believed the volunteers coped 'better than we anticipated.' She added: 'Of course, there have been ups and downs but overall they had a very positive experience.'

Daily Mail

COMPREHENSION

1 How many volunteers were there?
2 How did they obtain what they needed?
3 How could people contact Emma?
4 What did Emma do to stop herself going mad?
5 In what ways did the experiment affect Emma?
6 On the whole, how did Helen Petrie describe the feelings of the volunteers?

DISCUSSION

1 If you don't use the Internet, why not? Are you afraid of it, or don't you have any interest in it?

2 Do you use e mail at home and at work? How has it changed the way you communicate with people?

3 Do you use it for anything else, such as banking or booking holidays?

4 Do you think the Internet is more male-oriented (used more by men and aimed more at them)? If so, why is that?

5 What advantages does it have over other media, such as TV, magazines and newspapers?

6 Whose responsibility should it be to check exactly what material goes on the Internet? Should it be the government's or the companies who provide the service (Internet Service Providers)?

7 Have you ever used a chat room? Do you think they might be dangerous in any way? Why, why not?

8 Do you think that it is dangerous for certain people to have access to sexual and violent material on the Internet? Why?

9 How do you think the Internet will develop over the next few years?

 **AMMUNITION BOX**

Key words
proxy server *an Internet Service Provider that filters out some incoming content; some countries such as Singapore insist on this*
to censor *to remove material that is considered indecent, offensive or a threat to security*
web site *where people can find information about a certain topic*
home page *the first, guiding page of your site*
e mail *electronic mail*
chat rooms *a service where messages are written and exchanged*
download *to transfer data from a large computer system to a smaller one*

ACTIVITIES

A ✍ **Read the letter written to a newspaper advice column. Discuss possible solutions with a partner and then write a reply to the woman.**

Dear Miriam

MY husband's addicted to the Internet. Day and night he chats to an American woman, sometimes intimately. We've been married for 27 years and a few months ago he told me he wanted a divorce. I found out he's been sending flowers to this woman he met on the Internet and he intends to go over and visit her.

He's 50 and all my friends have told me he's probably going through a midlife crisis. He talks all the time to this woman. I know for sure he's not seeing anyone else, it's just the Internet that's got a stranglehold on him.

He's always been a bully and has threatened that if I did anything to get in touch with the woman, he'd set our two Alsatian dogs on me. What can I do?

Daily Mirror

B **Work in groups of four and debate the following issue: It is the responsibility of the individual to censor what he/she views on the Internet.**

" ... she'll get the kids, but I'll get our page on the Internet."

 **NETWORKING**

Find out how the Internet is controlled.

Book: *Rough Guide to the Internet* published by Rough Guides

Film: *The Net* (1995) directed by Irwin Winkler

Play: *Closer* by Patrick Marber

Websites:
www.profound.co.uk
www.hippy.freeserve.co.uk/censor/
www.birmingham.co.uk/english

 **FOCUS**

● What is your perception of Great Britain? How do you see British people? Are there any stereotypes of the British in your country?
● How do you think the British would like to be seen by other countries?

Dome sculptures shows bleak side of the British

By **Nicholas Hellen**
Media Correspondent

The Millennium Dome, London

We have come 2,000 years but visitors to the Millennium Dome may wonder what progress we have made.

A collection of larger-than-life sculptures will portray the grotesque characters who often dominate perceptions of modern British society. They include lager louts, football hooligans and fat-cat businessmen.

The works will be designed by Gerald Scarfe, who was asked to cast a critical eye over the evolution of the British character. His visions, to be displayed in the national identity zone of the Greenwich dome, will make a powerful contrast to the atmosphere of relentless optimism portrayed elsewhere within it. 'I have been given complete freedom

to show the British character as I see it,' he said this weekend. 'Although there will be some benign images, it is true to say that the exhibition will not show us in an entirely flattering light.'

It is a fair bet that many visitors will be brought up short by the shock of self-recognition. While much of the dome will be devoted to promoting the talents of the British media, Scarfe will show programmes spewing out of a screen in a torrent of filth, engulfing a slobbish male coach potato who is too lazy too move.

Tony Blair, the Prime Minister, has described the £758 million dome as a beacon of British excellence that will attract worldwide interest. By contrast, Scarfe will depict

patriotism in the degraded form of a human crouched on all fours like a British bulldog, with a flag instead of a head. Scarfe goes further: his Britain will be depicted as a land of inequality in which a businessman, dressed in trousers made of £20 notes, strides unfeelingly over a homeless person in a shelter made of shopping bags from Harrods and Fortnum & Mason.

Another installation will depict paparazzi, looking like flies on a dung heap, with flashing camera lenses for eyes, and a lager lout is depicted with an unwieldy beer barrel for a torso. Not all the characters are objectionable. Scarfe, who also brought Hercules, the mythical hero, to life for a blockbuster Disney animation, will show an

amiable John Bull holding a cricket bat and a sign for cream teas.

An opinion poll organised by Marks and Spencer, the sponsor of the zone, has yielded thousands of suggestions for images of British life that the public believe should be taken into the third millennium. Insiders say the list has been carefully compiled to satisfy separatist opinion in Scotland and Wales, as well as reflecting ethnic minorities. Pictures of Diana, Princess of Wales will occupy a prominent slot, although it is believed plans have been dropped to display her wedding dress. Other confirmed images include British newspapers, Scottish whisky, a red telephone box and a tea cosy.

THE SUNDAY TIMES

COMPREHENSION

1 Where will the sculptures be shown?
2 Who will they be designed by?
3 Name two of the 'qualities' Scarfe planned to portray.
4 Who have the organisers taken care not to offend?
5 How might the British react to the sculptures?

DISCUSSION

1 Why do you think the artist has shown the British like this?

2 How do you think the British will react to these sculptures?

3 If you have been to Britain, do you think they are fair representations? Why, why not?

4 How do you think your nation would be portrayed if there were an exhibition like this?

5 How accurate do you think national stereotypes are?

6 Do you think stereotypes can be harmful or dangerous? Why, why not?

7 What are your country's national stereotypes?

Baroness Thatcher by Gerald Scarfe

ACTIVITIES

A Role-play: The 'New Millennium, New World' project is looking for ideas for a travelling exhibition. You have been asked to design one of the exhibits. It could be something representing your country or the world, focussing on a theme such as culture, technology or history. The choice is yours! Work together in groups of four or five. Decide what exhibits there will be, and what kinds of activities you will provide for the visitors. If there is more than one group in the class, each can present its ideas and vote on which is the best.

B Imagine that you are a critic writing a review on one group's exhibition. Write about your experience and what you did and didn't enjoy. Remember to justify your opinions, and feel free to invent any extra details.

 NETWORKING

How do people view your country? What are the national stereotypes?

Books: *Anatomy of Britain* by Anthony Sampson
Notes From A Small Island by Bill Bryson
The English by Jeremy Paxman
The State We Are In by Will Hutton

Films: *Blue Murder at St Trinians* (1957) directed by Frank Lauder
Crocodile Dundee (1986) directed by Paul Hogan
Monsieur Hulot's Holiday (1953) directed by Jaques Tati
Mr Bean (1997) directed by Mel Smith
Pleasantville (1998) directed by Gary Ross
The Lavender Hill Mob (1951)directed by Charles Crichton

Website:
www.greenwich2000.co.uk

AMMUNITION BOX

Key words

Positive
patriotic *to support your country*
hospitable *welcoming*
artistic *having natural skill in the arts such as painting or dancing*
magnanimous *generous or forgiving, especially to an enemy or rival*
just *fair*

Negative
nationalistic *having a strong feeling of love and pride in one's country*
small minded *mean, not generous or forgiving*
parochial *narrow minded*
arrogant *to behave in a proud or superior manner*

FOCUS

- What do you think makes a story 'newsworthy'? What factors might make an editor decide *not* to publish a story?
- How much influence do newspapers have in your country?

On a Saturday in November a woman called Bridget, 30, left her London home to fly to Germany for a weekend break. Most people would think of Bridget as being middle class. After all, she was fairly well connected with friends and relatives in diplomatic circles.

A story nobody told

Roy Greenslade

While staying at the embassy in Bonn she met a young woman, who was also travelling on the Eurostar back to London. With encouragement from the ambassador, who was Bridget's cousin, she agreed to accompany her on the train. Their journey was uneventful until passport control in Brussels. Bridget's companion was travelling on a false passport and requested political asylum. Bridget was charged with attempting to smuggle the woman into the country. It was a clear error. But the Belgian authorities decided to proceed with the case. Bridget's distraught partner in England sought legal advice and was eventually introduced to Stephen Jakobi, director of Fair Trials Abroad.

He soon realised the problem and knew that the most potent weapon in such cases was publicity generated by newspapers. By the time Jakobi was alerted it was December 23rd, and he thought it was a perfect Christmas story.

One of his first calls was to the Press Association's respected correspondent Jo Butler, who quickly filed a story which turned up on every newsroom screen. But Bridget's plight didn't strike any editor as worthy of telling.

Butler filed a couple more stories, but to no avail. 'None of them were taken up. But I have to be honest, I wasn't surprised, black women don't make stories.'

Oh, yes, I had forgotten to mention that Bridget Seisay is a black woman with an African background. After five months in jail she was tried, convicted, and sentenced to three years in jail.

Written evidence of her innocence from Umaru Wurie, the Sierra Leone ambassador to Germany, was disregarded, as was the testimony of her asylum-seeking companion.

Jakobi says 'It was one of the worst miscarriages of justice I have seen.' He believes that racism was a major factor, claiming 'If Bridget had been white, she would have been released months ago.'

Jakobi is also convinced that racism is the reason Britain's press has failed to take up Bridget's case.

Compare her experience with that of Ruth Sandberg, arrested in Italy on a charge of smuggling cocaine. Once her family had alerted the British press,

several papers featured her case. It was, they said, an outrage. After she was sentenced to 11 years' jail, virtually every paper went into action before a court ruled that her conviction was unsafe because of irregularities.

The press support for Ruth, now back in Britain with her two children, echoes many other similar instances. But Bridget has had no such backing though her case has been taken up by *The Voice*, the paper that serves the black community.

News editor Garfield Myrie says: 'We took up Bridget's case because we believe she is innocent. What the white media do or don't do is for them to explain.' Indeed it is.

A privately owned profit-making press which depends on selling as many copies as possible is bound to reject material which editors believe might harm sales.

But what does it say about newspapers' claims to exist in the public interest? And what does it say about their claims to support a multi-cultural society?

The Guardian

COMPREHENSION

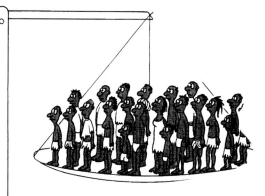

1 Where did Bridget go for a weekend break?
2 Where did she stay?
3 What did Stephen Jakobi think would help her plight?
4 Why weren't the newspapers interested in her story?
5 How was the case of Ruth Sandberg different?

DISCUSSION

1 Why do you think the newspapers ignored Bridget's story?

2 Do different races, communities and cultures get equal attention from the media in your country? Can you think of any examples?

3 Do certain communities have their own newspapers or magazines to represent their views?

4 Do you think that newspapers put profit before public interest? Can you think of any papers in your country that are different? Do they have a high readership?

5 In certain cases newspapers have been shown to influence their readers by biased reporting. Do you think this is wrong? Can you think of any actual examples?

6 How do you think newspapers can be made more accountable to the public about which stories they run? Is there an organisation in your country that monitors the press?

ACTIVITIES

A Role-play: A complaint has been made to the Press Complaints Commission about the papers not covering Bridget's story. Follow the instructions, then act out the situation in groups of three.

Press Complaints Commission (PCC):
You represent the Press Complaints Commission. A complaint has been made about the press not taking up Bridget Seisay's story. Bridget's lawyer claims that this is due to racism, and that a white woman in her position would have achieved greater press coverage. They are seeking compensation and an apology.

The newspaper editor:
You represent one of the biggest-selling broadsheets in the country. Your defence is that at the time the story broke there were other more important stories to cover. The paper has a non-racial policy and aims to cover as many stories as possible regardless of race. You also cite the fact that no other paper or television news programme covered the story. You need to give examples of stories your paper covered that dealt with different races.

The race-relations lawyer:
You believe that the lack of coverage directly affected Bridget's case. Had the newspapers done more, Bridget's case might have been heard earlier, or the Belgian authorities might have realised their error. You believe that the lack of coverage was due to Bridget being black, and you are seeking compensation for the time spent in prison in Belgium.

B Imagine you are Bridget's lawyer. Write a letter to a newspaper asking:

– Why it didn't cover Bridget's story

– Why it covered Ruth's story

Give your opinion on the importance of Bridget's story and the treatment of ethnic minorities in the media.

NETWORKING

Find out about the press in your country. Do a survey to find out what kinds of stories the papers cover – are there some groups and topics that seem to be excluded?

Books: *Beloved* by Toni Morrison
I Know Why The Caged Bird Sings by Maya Angelou
Race, Racism and Psychology by Graham Richards
Secrets of the Press by Stephen Glover

Film: *The Color Purple* (1985) directed by Steven Spielberg

Websites:
www.cre.gov.uk/
www.ebony.com
www.pcc.org.uk/
www.scandals.org
www.village.cossnet.co.uk

AMMUNITION BOX

Key words

tabloid *tabloid newspapers have pages half the size of larger papers and contain light or popular stories*
broadsheet *newspapers printed on a large size of paper. They usually contain more serious news items than tabloid papers*
to discriminate *to treat one person or group different to another*

Handy hints

• **Press Complaints Commission (PCC):** The PCC is an independent organisation set up in 1991 to ensure that British newspapers and magazines follow the letter and spirit of an ethical Code of Practice dealing with issues such as inaccuracy, privacy, misrepresentation and harassment. The commission resolves complaints about possible breaches of the code and gives guidance to editors on related ethical issues. Every year the PCC receives 3,000 complaints

 FOCUS
- Are you generally optimistic or pessimistic about the future?
- How many ways can you think of to predict the future?

Making predictions can be quite difficult – but here is some advice taken from the Internet on how to predict the future successfully!

Now you can become rich and famous by predicting the future, just follow the easy steps below:

- You don't have to believe your own predictions – in fact, doing so may distract you from your goal of becoming rich and famous.
- Above all, keep in mind that failed predictions are not news, but successful ones are. Even if only one in 50 of your predictions is on target, announce that to the media and send out press releases reminding everyone that you were right.
- Talk about upcoming major changes, without going into specific details. No matter which time period you are in, there are always major changes ahead.
- Keep in mind that the people who believe your predictions have a high chance of believing in astrology, UFOs and various new-age subjects, and have a fascination for ancient cultures, the pyramids, the origin of man, and other related subjects. Be sure to include those subjects in your predictions – it will increase your readers' interest in them.
- When possible, be vague in your predictions, so you can claim 'a hit', no matter what happens, for example, despite certain problems there will be a positive development in French politics.
- Predict several events that have a high probability of happening – ferry accidents in the Philippines, hurricanes in Florida, discoveries of new drugs, assassinations of politicians, scandals involving members of the British royal family or the Italian parliament and so on.
- Trust your readers not to follow every prediction you make. After the year is over, proudly list every prediction you count as a hit, and ignore those you miss, or claim that they will come true later.
- In general, avoid mentioning exact dates – the odds are against you, but if you do so, leave a loophole. For example: 'The Awareness says the probability is high that a major earthquake will strike southern Iceland, possibly in July. The event might take place on July 3rd, at 8:21am, but if the spiritual developments in the area are sufficiently positive this event might be delayed for as much as a few years'. If you get the prediction exactly right, you will become famous the world over. If you are close enough, claim this as a hit. If you are way off, take the loophole exit, and if necessary claim that this will become true later.

http://www.complex.is/asylum/success.html

 COMPREHENSION

1. Is it important to believe you are telling the truth when predicting the future?
2. How much information should you give?
3. What kind of people might believe your predictions?
4. What kind of events should you try to predict?
5. What does the writer mean by a 'loophole exit'?
6. Why do earthquakes make such a good subject for predictions?

 DISCUSSION

1 Do you believe it is possible to predict the future? How?

2 Do you think people who say they can predict the future are telling the truth?

3 Nostradamus made a famous series of predictions. Are there any famous prophets in your country? Do you know any of their prophecies? Have any of these come true?

4 Another way of looking at the future is by looking at the past: what do you think is meant by the saying 'History repeats itself'? Do you agree with it?

5 Why do you think people who predict the future are treated with such scepticism?

6 Do you think ancient ways of predicting the future, such as astrology, should be taken seriously?

ACTIVITIES

A **In groups of two or three, imagine you have been asked to advise future generations on conducting your country's affairs and the state of the world. What events would you use to illustrate important points? What might be the most important issues for the future? Share your ideas with the rest of the class.**

B ✍ **Write an essay: The next hundred years are likely to be far worse than the last hundred years. Do you agree? Give reasons for your answers.**

AMMUNITION BOX

Key words

mystic *someone who tries to be united with God, and through that reach truths beyond human understanding*

sceptic *someone who doubts that a claim is true*

prophet *someone who claims to be able to see into the future, especially the future of the world*

fortune teller *someone who sees into people's future*

Handy hints

- Nostradamus (1503-1566) became famous with the publication of *Centuries*, in which he made a number of prophecies. Some of his prophecies include:
- The French Revolution
- The rise of Hitler, referred to as 'Hister'
- The assassination of the US president John F. Kennedy

Astrology was first developed by the Chaldeans and the Babylonians. The word zodiac was coined later by the Greeks and translates as Circle of Animals.

 NETWORKING

Find out more about famous soothsayers from around the world. When did they live and what events did they predict?

Books: *Brave New World* by Aldous Huxley
1984 by George Orwell

Films: *2001: A Space Odyssey* (1968) directed by Stanley Kubrick
Back to the Future (1985) directed by Robert Zemeckis
Star Wars (1977) directed by George Lucas
Terminator (1984) directed by James Cameron
The Fifth Element (1997) directed by Luc Besson
Twelve Monkeys (1995) directed by Terry Gilliam

Websites:
cccw.adh.bton.ac/uk
www2.eridu.co.uk/

- Think of five cartoon superheroes and write them down on a piece of paper. For example, Superman.
- Look at the names again. How many of those characters are *not* Caucasians (are not white)? How many are Asian or African, for example? How many *don't* show typical Caucasian features?

Why Don't Asia's Heroes Look Asian? *BY NURY VITTACHI*

Come with me to a place where many of the deepest, darkest, innermost thoughts on the super-sensitive subject of race are hidden. The place is the comic-book section of the street-side newsstand.

This is a pet interest of mine, for two reasons. First, I once worked as a cartoonist myself. Second, while fate has given me the coffee-colored skin of a South Asian, my wife has the milk-tea look of a Caucasian and my adopted children the vanilla-latte appearance of the Chinese.

In modern societies, we say all races are considered equal. But we are lying. I spend most of my time in Asia, and our comic books reveal what we really think on the subject: Caucasians are superior, and we want to be like them.

Ouch! No! This cannot be true. It would be too painful. But let me show you the evidence. Every comic on the newsstand outside my office in Hong Kong depicts heroes with round eyes, straight European noses and fair hair.

In Tokyo, similar rules hold true. Comic heroes are tall, round-eyed, straight-nosed and often blond. Japanese artists frequently draw eyes as oval orbs and they often ink in only the bridge of the nose, ignoring the nostrils. These techniques make the faces as Caucasian as possible.

The comic-book racial differences between South Asians and Caucasians are more subtle, but artists still make the necessary adjustments. Rarely in South Asian comics – or in the movies – will you find dark brown skin or the big,

expressive Indian nose. I am in no way suggesting that this is a form of conscious racism forced upon us by Caucasians. We do it to ourselves, and we do it unconsciously.

Over the years, I have found only one group of artists that regularly tries to put accurate racial characteristics into their drawings of Asians. Plaudits, please, to the unsung doodlers of a multinational firm not usually credited with great cultural sensitivity: the Walt Disney Co. I cheer because Aladdin has a big, hooked nose – like some of my Arab friends. In *The Lion King*, set in Africa, Mufasa has wide, flared nostrils and a hot chocolate voice. Of course, Disney doesn't always get it right: Mulan's eyes, for example, are way too steeply angled. But Disney tries – unlike us here in Asia.

Contemplating this issue has led me to consider a question other Asians may already have asked themselves: All things being equal, would I prefer to be Caucasian? Yes, I reply, shocking myself. All men want to be heroes. All heroes are Caucasian. End of argument.

In the meantime, my five-year-old is progressing well with his reading. The other day, I laid a bunch of comic books from around the world in front of him and asked which character he most identified with. He chose a talking beetle called Dim, from *A Bug's Life*, 'because he has blue skin and six legs.' But that's a kid for you. Long may he remain racially color-blind.

TIME

COMPREHENSION

1 Why is the writer interested in this subject (two reasons)?
2 What, according to the author, do Asian comic books reveal about Asian attitudes to race?
3 How do Hong Kong cartoonists make their characters look Caucasian?
4 Who is responsible for this form of racism?
5 Who makes the greatest effort to portray racially accurate characters?
6 Why does the writer say his five-year-old is racially colour-blind?

 **DISCUSSION**    **ACTIVITIES**

1 Is it important that cartoon characters should accurately reflect their racial origins? Why, why not?

2 How important do you think cartoons are as a medium for shaping children's opinions and ideas?

3 How about comic books from your country – do the heroes look Caucasian?

4 Why do you think the characters are drawn as Western Europeans? Is it a conscious decision by cartoonists? Could it be the influence of so much US culture?

5 Do you think Walt Disney cartoon characters such as Aladdin and Mulan accurately portray their racial roots? What about their accents – are they too American, or is this necessary as the films are made for an American audience?

6 Why do you think the writer said he would prefer to be Caucasian? Was he being serious? Would you like to be of a different race? If so, why?

7 How can people be encouraged to produce more cartoons/movies portraying their own racial types? Or should we give the audience what it wants, regardless of the content?

A **Work in groups of three or four. A satellite TV channel has asked for proposals for a new cartoon series.**
You need to keep these points in mind:

- The series, though made in English, is to be broadcast in Asia, and may be sold to Africa or Latin America
- The target audience is young adults, ideally both girls and boys
- There needs to be a chance to produce merchandise associated with the series

Provide details of the characters, heroes and villains, and a little of their personal history.

B ✒ **Write an essay: Why do people need heroes? Who, besides fictional characters such as Superman, are considered superheroes in your country?**

 AMMUNITION BOX

Key words
subconscious *concerning thoughts, fears, instincts of which one is not fully aware but which influence one's actions*
to portray *to describe someone/something in words or a picture*
to reflect a society *to give an image of a society (how do these comics reflect Asian society?)*
stereotype *an image or idea that has become fixed in a conventional form without any individuality*

Handy hints
- The Phantom made his debut on February 17th 1936 and was the first costumed comic-book hero
- In June 1938, *Action Comics #1* came out, featuring a man in a red and blue costume lifting a car over his head! This was Superman, the very first comic character to have powers far beyond those of a normal human being
- *Detective Comics #27* hit the stands in May 1939. In it we saw the first appearance of Batman. The very first sidekick came out in April 1940. His name was Robin the Boy Wonder. He first appeared in *Detective Comics #38*
- The first *Superman* film was made in 1978 starring Christopher Reeve as the superhero
- The first *Batman* film directed by Tim Burton was made in 1989 starring Michael Keaton

 **NETWORKING**

Find out about superheroes in your country. Is the superhero an entirely American idea?

Books: *The Encyclopedia of Animated Cartoons* by Jeff Lenburg
Cartoons and Animation by Ivan Bullock

Films: *Batman* (1989) directed by Tim Burton
Superman (1978) directed by Richard Donner

Websites:
www.comic-art.com
www.disney.co.uk/
www.geocitiessucks.com/

1.   2.

FOCUS

- How common is it for children to come from single-parent families in your country?
- How are single parents viewed by your society?

Single out the selfish breeders

Sue Carroll

We've topped the European league this year. Our teenager pregnancy rate – around 90,000 a year in England alone – is six times higher than in Holland (one of the most sexually liberated nations on earth), and four times higher than in France.

What a sorry state. And what exactly have we done? Nothing, other than to pat these girls on the head, make sure they're comfortably housed, then provide enough money so that they can gaze in wonderment at the rest of us mere mortals getting out of bed every morning to earn a decent living.

Criminal

This attitude of complacency is criminal. And it's got to stop. Tony Blair proposes to change the law so that under-18 teenage mothers will be housed in semi-supervised accommodation.

I couldn't care whether they stick them in the slammer so long as it gets them off the benefit bandwagon.

It's OK, I'm braced for the countless letters I'll receive from the bleeding hearts who believe I belong back in the Dark Ages where becoming a single mother was a stigma. But rather that than a society which bends over backwards to tolerate the likes of 19-year-old Samantha Dawson, who has four children by three fathers and wants more. A girl who repeatedly boasts: 'People are talking a load of rubbish when they complain about what unmarried mothers get. We need it and we are entitled to it. I make sure my children get the best of everything. Why shouldn't they just because I don't work?'

It's enough to make your teeth grind. God only knows what job she'll make of dragging up her own brood. The real tragedy is that Samantha is not an isolated case. Figures released reveal that numbers are increasing, and though there will always be a few genuine hard luck cases who really need the welfare state, the majority are frighteningly similar to her. Girls who, because rents will be covered, will never learn the true meaning of the word self-respect. What chance does that give their own children?

I'm sick of the finger pointing moralists who claim that these girls are victims of inner-city life, so desperate to leave unhappy homes that the only escape route they understand comes in the shape of a newborn babe. This is not the only way out but the easiest. Countless men and women have lived in circumstances beyond endurance and managed to emerge without fleecing every other taxpayer in the land.

Aware

Holier than thou anti-sex education evangelists like Ann Widdecombe believe that children are more sexually aware because they know too much too young. She'd be better getting her knickers in a twist over what they don't learn, vital lessons about life and responsibility. I knew about sex when I was 10 years old. Had I been even remotely interested I wouldn't have done it. Why? Because I'd have been too damned scared. The way teenage girls will be when they face the fact that from now on – we hope – having a baby no longer paves the way to the pampered life of a protected species.

Mirror

COMPREHENSION

1 What is the teenage pregnancy rate in England?
2 How will the law change?
3 Why does Samantha Dawson think teenage mothers should get money?
4 What's the writer's opinion on the argument that having a baby is the only way out for these girls?

DISCUSSION

1 How well do you think a single parent can bring up a child?

2 Do you think children from single-parent families suffer because of it?

3 What problems do you think single parents face? How can they overcome these problems?

4 Do you think the state should be responsible for helping single parents? If so, how?

5 Do you think people should be able to have as many children as they want?

6 Should single parents have priority for receiving housing? Why, why not?

7 Many mothers are abandoned by the child's father. How can absent fathers be made to face up to their responsibilities? How much maintenance should they pay and should they be punished if they refuse?

8 In the UK, the number of single mothers is increasing. How do you think this can be prevented? Better sex education at school? Tougher laws for absent fathers?

9 Can single fathers be as good at parenting as single mothers?

 **ACTIVITIES**

A Role-play: Work in groups of three. Lisa Rowe, aged 19, has just had a baby. At present she and the child are living with her parents. However, she has applied to the local council for a flat as the situation at home has become very difficult. Students A and B must present their ideas to the judge, who will make a decision.

Student A
You are Lisa's lawyer. Your client was going to train to become a teacher until she got pregnant. The pregnancy was unplanned, but Lisa is very happy to be a mother. However, she is now unemployed, and doesn't want to continue living with her parents as they opposed the pregnancy and their house is too cramped. You want the council to provide a two-bedroom flat for Lisa. Make the best case you can to ensure Lisa gets a flat.

Student B
You are the council's lawyer. The council already has a long list of people waiting to be rehoused, and you believe that as Lisa is in secure accommodation at the moment, hers is not an urgent case. Put the council's view forward as best you can, inventing any other details you might need.

Student C
You are the judge who has been appointed to decide the case. Listen to both lawyers, ask any questions you need to, and allow them to question one another. Then make the decision as to whether Lisa will be rehoused.

As a class compare the deals you made and decide who was the best lawyer!

B ✍ Write a short report on the case you have just heard. Summarise the points made by each lawyer and the judgement made.

Or

✍ Write a letter in response to the article, either agreeing with the points the writer made or presenting the other point of view.

 AMMUNITION BOX

Key words
contraception *methods used to deliberately prevent a woman becoming pregnant*
ante-natal care *care for pregnant women before the birth*
sex education *when young boys and girls are taught about sex and reproduction*
family planning *the process of planning the number of children, intervals between births by using birth control*

Handy hints
- 87% of the 41,000 babies born to 15-19-year-olds in Britain were outside marriage. This compares with 62% in the United States and 10% in Japan*
- The survey of 53 countries showed that Britain has one of the highest rates of sexual activity in the world among teenagers and young women
- About 10% of women in Britain are married by the time they are 18. For the US the figure is 11%, Brazil 24% and Ghana 38%
- Britain is known to have the highest teenage pregnancy rate in Europe. The London boroughs of Lambeth, Lewisham and Southwark have the most teenage pregnancies in England, with 10% pregnant by the time they are 20
- Teenage mothers are more likely to drop out of school than girls who have a child later. A teenage mother will lack job skills, making it hard for her to find a job
- Teenage mothers may not have developed good parenting skills or have the social support system to help them raise a child

* Source: *1999 Survey of Sexual Activity in Young Women*, The Alan Guttmacher Institute, New York

 **NETWORKING**

Find out about the number of single parents in your country. How does the state help them?

Book: *Single and Lone Parents* by Craig Donnellan

Films: *Big Daddy* (1999) directed by Dennis Dugan
Three Men And A Little Lady (1990) directed by Emile Ardolino
Nil By Mouth (1997) directed by Gary Oldman

Websites:
www.ippf.org/newsinfo/index.htm
www.noah.cuny.edu/pregnancy

◎ **FOCUS**
- What kind of holidays do you enjoy?
- How much interest do you take in the culture of a foreign country when you visit?

A lonely planet? Not remotely

Round the world traveller *Emily Barr* on the predictability of backpacking

The woman on the platform at New Delhi station took one look at us. 'You're going to Dharamsala,' she said. 'You people always go there.' Fifteen hours later, we realised what she meant. The town which for 40 years has been the home of the exiled Tibetan community is now packed with westerners. Everyone caters for the backpacker, because these are the people who, relatively speaking, have money.

I spent the past six months in Asia, and I have no idea why Dr Aziz of the Roehampton Institute took two years to uncover the shocking fact that backpackers hang out with each other, speak English and eat western food, when a half a day in McLeodganj or Bangkok would have proved the point.

The sad truth is that backpacking is a painfully predictable affair; all the stereotypes are true. The Khao San Road in Bangkok and similar ghettos elsewhere are packed with people who think they are seeing Asia, while they eat a banana pancake and reminisce about the lovely espresso in Krabi. Backpackers are tourists – the differences between them and package tourists are choice of destination, length of trip, and the amount of money spent.

Cities such as Bangkok and Kathmandu can absorb these ghettos easily. They provide amusement for the locals (many make expeditions to look at the visitors) and home comforts for the tourists. Smaller places, however, have their characters irreversibly changed by invasion by gallumphing hordes in backpacks.

The chief culprits for these kinds of changes are the *Lonely*

Backpackers on a mountain path

Planet guides. These books are ubiquitous in Asia, as I discovered on my third day in Vietnam when, on a trip to the Mekong Delta, the guide apologetically announced that, although we would be visiting a floating market, 'it is not the one in The Book'. *Lonely Planet* books cover every square inch of Asia. They are the most popular guidebooks with young backpackers, partly because their information is clear and accurate, but mostly because these are the books that everyone else has, and young people travelling for the first time do not want to be left out. The guidebooks make and break guesthouses and restaurants. More importantly, they send young travellers to remote places they would not otherwise get to, and the places inevitably lose the qualities that made them so attractive.

Not all the blame can be laid at the door of Tony Wheeler, *Lonely Planet*'s boss. In Vang Vieng, I sat at a bar with a cold beer, watching the sun set. About 50 other westerners were doing the same thing. Behind me an argument was raging: 'But in north London you've got a much better Tube network. In south London, you might as well be in Brighton.' Business as usual, in other words.

One failsafe method is to go somewhere where there is neither the poverty nor the interest in the west that makes places pander to Europeans. China, for example. Thailand is more of a challenge; but there are places, even in south east Asia, where it is possible to get away from tourism. I only came across a few of them. As for where they are, that would be telling.

The Guardian

COMPREHENSION
1 How long did the writer spend in Asia?
2 What does the writer think about backpacking?
3 What's the prime reason young people get the *Lonely Planet* guidebooks?
4 What effect have these guidebooks had on both the backpackers and the places they visit?
5 Why do China and similar places offer more to the *real* traveller who wants to get away from it all?

DISCUSSION

1 Have you ever been backpacking? If so, what has been your experience?

2 Do you think the writer's criticisms are fair or unfair? What kind of a traveller do you think she is?

3 Do you have many tourists where you live? If so, what is your opinion of them?

4 Do tourists ruin the quiet places they go to see? Can you think of any examples from your own experience?

5 Should certain sites be put 'out of bounds' to tourists? What are the arguments for and against this? Which point of view do you hold?

6 What advantages does tourism bring? What disadvantages? Do the advantages outweigh the disadvantages, or vice-versa?

7 How much can/do tourists learn about the country they are visiting?

"Hi it's me. I'm on a camel train."

ACTIVITIES

A Role-play: The quiet town of Seaville is on the coast of your country. It is an old town that has remained unspoilt. However, there is a big unemployment problem. Recently a holiday company has approached the town council with a view to developing the town as a tourist destination. The following research has been carried out by the council:

- 60% of the townspeople are against the tourist plans. However, amongst the young, 85% approve of it. They would get most jobs and they have the highest unemployment
- Those who are against the plan might vote you out of office!
- The holiday company wants to build a massive hotel. Police say that the crime rate would probably rise, and it would have an effect on the environment. Against this, the extra money would allow the town to build a hospital and other public facilities
- The holiday company also wants to build nightclubs and pubs. Again, the young are for this, and the old are against!
- If the holiday company doesn't get its way, it may not invest in your town

Student A, take the part of a town council representative.
Student B, take the role of a holiday company representative.
Students C and D, take the role of two people who live in the village: one is against the plans, the other supports them.

Each person needs to present his/her case, and Student A has to decide whether to go ahead with the proposal or not. Be prepared to justify your decision to the people of your town (young and old) as well as the holiday company.

B Using the ideas you discussed above, write up your decision.

AMMUNITION BOX

Key words
backpacker *a person who travels with a backpack*
to spoil *to ruin*
environment *natural surroundings*
idyllic *perfect*
tranquil *quiet*
hordes of *many*
character *what makes a place distinct or special*
to overrun *to completely fill a place*

Handy hints
In reply to the article, the *Lonely Planet* organisation makes the following points:

- The guides were only for places with the necessary tourist infrastructure
- The guidebooks contain information on cultural and ethical issues to allow travellers to make informed decisions
- The writers are aware of their influence and write responsibly to help travellers to make informed decisions
- Tourism can bring great economic rewards. Exposure of a country to the outside world, as well as fear of losing tourist revenues, can be a reason for reform
- The search for the tourist dollar can override important issues such as the environment. Money can be diverted to provide tourist resources at the cost of helping native inhabitants

NETWORKING

Find out how tourism has affected your country.

Books: *An Accidental Tourist* by Anne Tyler
The Beach by Alex Garland

Films: *The Beach* (2000) directed by Danny Boyle

Websites:
www.holidaybank.co.uk/tourops/eco.htm
www.iipt.org/
www.lonelyplanet.com

 **FOCUS**

The study of infertility has made enormous progress over the past two or three decades, but its success has been accompanied by new problems.
- What treatments are now available for infertile couples?
- What problems might arise from these treatments?

Black and white test-tube twins shock for mum

From BARRY WIGMORE in New York

A WHITE mum gave birth to black and white twin boys after a test-tube bungle at a fertility clinic. Shocked Donna Fassano's white baby is her own natural child by hubby Richard.

His black 'brother' was born because embryos from another patient, black Debbie Rogers, were mistakenly implanted in Donna's womb along with her own fertilised eggs.

Donna wanted to keep both babies. But after being threatened with legal action, she has agreed to hand over the black tot to Debbie and

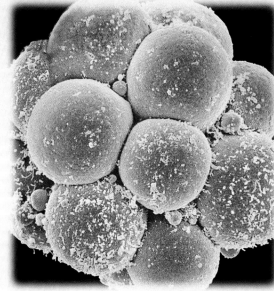
16-cell embryo

husband Robert. Debbie lost her own test-tube babies in a miscarriage.

Donna said: 'We want what's in our son's best interests – that's why we are giving him up. But it's tearing me apart.' Both couples went to the New

York clinic of fertility expert Dr Lillian Nash after trying for a baby for years.

They paid £1,000 each to have eggs extracted from the wives' ovaries and fertilised in test tubes by the husbands' sperm.

The mix-up happened

when the two women returned to the clinic to have their fertile eggs transferred to their wombs.

After realising what had happened, Dr Nash, 71, alerted both women when Donna was three months pregnant. But because multiple embryos were implanted and only two survived, it was impossible to predict the babies' colour until their birth three months ago.

Heartbroken Donna, who refuses to reveal the boys' names, will hand over the black twin if DNA tests prove Debbie and Robert are his natural parents. Both couples plan to sue Dr Nash.

Donna said: 'Who cares what colour my little boy is? I carried him, gave birth to him, and loved him. Now I feel I am losing him. But I understand how this woman must feel because I know what it's like to be childless.'

Debbie's lawyer Rudolph Silas said: 'I phoned her last night with the news. She and Robert were excited and overwhelmed. Their house was full of joy — and lots of tears.'

The Sun

COMPREHENSION

1 Which child is the biological child of Donna Fassano?
2 What did Donna originally plan to do with her black child?
3 What final test must Debbie and Robert take before receiving their child?
4 Why did Donna feel she had a right to keep her black child?

AMMUNITION BOX

Key words
IVF in vitro *fertilisation; where the egg is fertilised in a test tube* (in vitro *means in glass*)
surrogate mother *a woman who has a baby on behalf of someone unable to have children*
embryo *a young animal or plant in the early stages of its development before birth*
midwife *a person, usually a woman, who assists in childbirth*
obstetrics *(obstetrician) branch of medicine and surgery concerned with childbirth*
gynaecology *(gynaecologist) the scientific study and treatment of diseases and disorders of the female reproductive system*

Handy hints
- Only 15% of IVF treatment is successful
- 18% of IVF treatment is NHS (government) funded in Britain
- Private treatment costs up to £2,000 for one cycle; most couples have three cycles, spending £3,420
- 1-2% of women have multiple births; with IVF, the odds rise to 25%

IVF: The facts

Around 6,000 babies a year are born in the UK to otherwise infertile couples as a result of in vitro fertilisation. But the techniques used often arouse huge controversy and some say the process can falsely raise would-be parents' hopes since it only has a success rate of around 15%.

What is IVF?

- IVF was developed in the 1970s. The first British test tube baby was Louise Brown, who was born in 1977
- Some 30,000 test tube babies have been born in the UK since then
- There are several different techniques, but the main process involves the woman taking fertility drugs to help her produce more eggs
- The eggs are then harvested and fertilised in the laboratory
- The woman is given hormone drugs to prepare her womb to receive the fertilised eggs
- The fertilised eggs are placed inside the womb and a normal pregnancy follows

www.news.bbc.co.uk

COMPREHENSION

1 How many babies are born a year as a result of *in vitro* fertilisation?
2 What is the success rate?
3 What is the process of *in vitro* fertilisation?

ACTIVITIES

A Role-play: Work in groups of four or five. Imagine that you are the managers at a city hospital. Appoint one student as your chairperson.

You have received this memo:

MEMO

Two mothers, Patient A and Patient B, received IVF treatment at this hospital 11 years ago. The treatment was successful and the offspring, Child A and Child B, are both now 10 years old. However, during the process, the embryos were accidentally swapped by mistake: this has only recently come to light. Child A is highly intelligent, her parents are university lecturers and are fairly well-off.
Child B was born severely handicapped and lives with his mother in a small flat. The parents divorced mainly due to the stress of caring for Child B. He has cost thousands of pounds, requires constant attention, and his mother is living on government benefit.

This error has only just been discovered, but neither the parents nor the press have any idea of the mix-up. If we decide to make this public, we may be sued for hundreds of thousands of pounds, and the adverse publicity from the press will harm the hospital. If, on the other hand, we keep quiet, there will be no payout, and no distress will be caused to the families concerned.

Discuss the memo and try to come to an agreement on a course of action. Bear in mind the best interests of the children and the families, and the hospital's legal and moral obligations. Then compare your solution with the other groups'.

B Imagine that a doctor who worked at the hospital leaked the story to the press. Write up the story. You can invent the details and use quotes from the people involved such as the doctor who leaked the story, the nurses and the parents. Use the first text to help you with the style of the piece.

DISCUSSION

1 Should background factors, such as age, marital status and job, affect who is given infertility treatment? If so, what criteria do you think should be used and who should make the final decision?

2 Who do you think should pay for the treatment – the couple or the government?

3 Do you think it is wrong that people who harm their health through smoking and drinking receive free hospital treatment, yet couples who through no fault of their own cannot have children, have to pay for their treatment? Give your reasons.

4 Do you think it is everyone's right to have children? Why, why not?

5 Should parents who already have children still have the right to infertility treatment? What if they remarry and have a new partner who is infertile?

6 What problems could arise if one parent was biological but the other one wasn't? How would you feel in these circumstances as the child? As the parent?

7 How possible – or likely – do you think it is that in the future, men and/or machines will carry children?

NETWORKING

Find out more about infertility treatment. What are people's attitudes towards it?

Books: *Inconceivable* by Ben Elton
The Longing by Jane Asher

Websites:
www.ein.org/
www.fuzz.com/nccm/10.htm
www.issue.co.uk

FOCUS

- What parts of the body can be used in transplants?
- What do you think of using animal organs for transplants?

Transplants from animals raise question of spreading disease

In 1993, an official with the Centre for Disease Control and Prevention (CDC) called a few employees into her office and asked the question: What was the CDC doing about the risk that animal-to-people transplants might introduce new germs into the human population? 'My first reaction was – nothing,' recalled Louisa Chapman, an expert on animal viruses that infect humans. 'Transplants from animals were so rare and recipients lived so briefly that it didn't seem a threat.'

But as she looked into the situation, she changed her mind. Interest in xenotransplants was heating up. Animals could not only ease the shortage of kidneys, hearts and livers for transplantation, but also supply brain tissue for treating diseases like Parkinson's. These days, drug and biotech companies have poured more than $100 million into xenotransplant research. Scientists report progress in overcoming rejection of animal organs. But the concern Chapman heard in that 1993 meeting has not gone away: Would xenotransplants give new germs a sneaky entrée into the human population?

In March, scientists at the Institute of Cancer Research in London reported that a virus – one that might be found even in healthy pigs – sprang out of pig tissue and infected human cells in a lab experiment. That showed that the idea of such infection in a pig-to-human transplant 'is more plausible than a fanciful scare story,' the researchers said. And federal regulators in the United States are now refining draft guidelines to minimise the risk to public health.

Here's why Chapman and others say there's reason to worry:

- Animals <u>do</u> have germs that can infect people and then spread from person-to-person.
- The AIDS virus apparently came from monkeys long ago.
- Dangerous germs can hide in healthy-looking animals.
- People getting animal organs would be on drugs to suppress their immune systems.
- Genes from an animal virus could mingle with those of a human virus, creating a hybrid virus with unpredictable behaviour.
- Keeping animals isolated from infection may not be enough. Some viruses aren't caught, they're inherited. They're just part of being a pig, for example.

So far, however, the limited experience with xenotransplants is encouraging. Dr Alan Dimick, who's put pigskin on severe burns since 1970, says there's no evidence treatment has infected anybody with pig germs. But Dimick notes that pigskin stays on for only a day or two. An implanted organ might pose more of a risk, he said.

Transgenic pigs which may provide donor organs for humans.

Dr James M. Schumacher, a neurosurgeon who has put foetal pig tissue into the brains of a dozen people with Parkinson's or Huntington's disease over the past two years, also reports no sign of infection. 'We are extremely overzealous about studying these effects and looking for viruses in the long and short run, and we haven't to date found any problem,' he said. While scientists ponder the risk of xenotransplantation, thousands of people die each year because they can't get a human organ.

'It's a difficult issue,' said virus expert Jonathan Allan. 'There are people dying. You want to do everything possible to prevent that. But you certainly don't want to foster new infectious diseases that would make even greater suffering in the population.'

BBC News Online

COMPREHENSION

1 What was Louisa Chapman's first reaction to the risk of animal transplants?
2 Why did she feel animal transplants weren't a threat?
3 Why did she change her mind?
4 How could animal transplants be used?
5 What are the possible dangers of animal to human transplant?
6 What is Dr Schumacher's opinion?

 **DISCUSSION**

1 How can people be encouraged to become organ donors? For what reasons might people not wish to donate their organs?

2 Pigs are now being genetically manipulated to carry human genes. Do you think this is ethical? Why, why not?

3 What possible alternatives do you think there are to using animal transplants?

4 Having read the article, do you think animal transplants seem too risky? Why, why not?

5 Who should make the decision to go ahead with research into animal transplants – doctors, lawyers, politicians?

6 Most research is being done by commercial pharmaceutical and biotechnology companies. One estimate suggests a potential market of $5 billion for sales of drugs associated with animal transplants. Do you think other organisations should be doing the research? Why, why not?

7 In what other ways do animals help the advance of human medicine? Should we continue to use them? Do animals have any rights themselves?

8 Would you be happy to receive an animal's organ if you were seriously ill?

9 What social and ethical problems do you think animal transplants raise?

AMMUNITION BOX

Key words

ethics *the moral issues, what is right and what is wrong*

donor *someone who agrees to give an organ to someone else*

rejection *when the patient's body attacks the new organ*

primate *a member of the most highly developed order of mammals*

immune system *the system in the body which helps the body fight disease*

Handy hints

- At the end of June 1999, 5,817 patients in the UK were waiting for a kidney transplant
- In 1998 there were 1,589 kidney transplants
- Each year there are fewer than 1,000 organ donors: this figure is rising at 3.3% a year
- 4.5 million people in Britain have registered as potential donors
- The organs and tissues most frequently required are corneas, heart valves, bone and skin
- Around 70% of the UK population are willing to donate their organs, but only 20% carry donor cards. Other countries have improved the supply of organs by adopting a system whereby it is presumed that people consent to donate their organs unless they actively opt out
- Some religions, such as Jehovah's Witnesses, refuse transplants of any kind

 **ACTIVITIES**

A Role-play: You are on the board of hospital trustees. You have to decide what to do about the following situation: There are three patients waiting for a kidney transplant. Each one shares the same unusual blood type – suitable human donors appear very rarely. A doctor in your hospital has claimed he can save one of these men with a trial animal transplant. Each patient has given his consent, but no-one yet knows the consequences of carrying out the operation. It could be a medical triumph or it could introduce a new plague into humanity!

You have to decide the following:

- Whether to agree to the animal transplant, or hope that a suitable human donor will be found
- Which patient will undergo the operation

Robert Kerr. White male aged 43. Waiting for nine months. Editor of the local newspaper (could be a useful connection!). This patient is quite unwell.

Isaac Jacobs Afro-Caribbean aged 49. Waiting for four months. Unmarried and no children. Seriously ill – doctors fear if he doesn't get a transplant in the next few days, he could die.

Saeed Jamal. Asian male aged 57. Waiting for 13 months but condition stable. Married, five children, three grandchildren – Saeed is main breadwinner for family. His wife is complaining about the wait, saying the hospital is racist, and may go to the press.

 **NETWORKING**

Find out more about animal transplants and the ethical problems related to them.

Books: *Organ Transplants and Ethics* (Avebury Series in Philosophy) by David Lamb
The Ethics of Organ Transplants: The Current Debate by Arthur L. Caplan

Film: *The Deep Blue Sea* (1999) directed by Renny Harlin

Websites:
wired.dcs.st-and.ac.uk
www.uncaged.co.uk/xtcdec.html

In groups, discuss the problem. When you have come to a decision, compare it with other groups'.

B Imagine you are the editor of a newspaper. Write an editorial (an opinion article) discussing the ethics of animal transplants, or write about the case above. Give your newspaper's opinion on what has happened.

 **FOCUS**

- Do you think girls are as aggressive as boys?
- Why do you think girls are becoming more violent?

Girls are turning to violent crime

Philip Johnston, Home Affairs Editor

Girls commit more than one in four of all juvenile crimes and are becoming increasingly involved in violence, according to a Government study published yesterday.

In 1957, girls accounted for only one crime in 11. This striking change was highlighted in a report into anti-social behaviour in adolescents. It shows that the criminal activities of so-called girl gangs are part of a worsening trend.

Over the past 10 years, the number of arrests of girls for violence has more than doubled and juvenile crime is increasing at a faster rate among girls than boys. This is said to be almost entirely the result of the post-war period – particularly family breakdown – that is evident across the western world.

In the past, girls were effectively supervised and were less likely to be exposed to anti-social influences. Anne Hagell, one of the authors of the report, said: 'Parents are less likely to supervise daughters as they once did. Young girls are spending increasing amounts of time at school. Also, where once a 13-year-old would sit in her own bedroom listening to records with a friend, now there is a trend towards girls doing the same as boys have always done, which is going around on the streets in groups of five or more.'

Boys are more likely to be involved in burglary and drug offences but the ratio falls for criminal damage, robbery, violence and theft.

The report says that poor parental supervision is a major factor in delinquency and the increase both in juvenile crime and the involvement of girls has coincided with high divorce rates and family breakdown. There is also a vicious circle at play, with anti-social girls more likely to become teenage mothers and to be less in a position to give their own offspring the care and that can prevent the next generation sliding into criminality.

The Daily Telegraph

COMPREHENSION

1 How many juvenile crimes are committed by girls?
2 In the past ten years, how has the number of juvenile arrests altered?
3 What reasons are put forward for girls becoming more violent?
4 What sort of crimes are boys involved in?

AMMUNITION BOX

Key words
delinquency *minor crimes committed by young people*
vicious circle *a state of affairs where the cause produces an effect which then produces the original cause*
surveillance *careful watch of someone suspected of doing wrong*
parental supervision *when parents keep check on their children*
family breakdown *when a mother and father split up*

Handy hints
- The peak age for offending among boys in Britain has risen from 13 in 1931 to 14 in 1971 and 18 today
- The peak age for offending among girls was 19 in 1938 and is now 15
- In the 14-25 age group 55% of males and 31% of females said they had committed at least one crime in their life
- There are 17 young-offender institutes for boys in Britain, but none for girls

Parents fit secret cameras to spy on their children

American parents are bugging their children's telephones, installing secret cameras in clock radios and sending strands of hair retrieved from pillows for analysis at drug laboratories.

They are resorting to Cold War espionage techniques and science to fight drug and alcohol abuse, which many turned into a way of life during their hippy days a generation ago.

Baby Boomers are hiring companies to bring sniffer dogs into their homes to track down traces of dope. Radio shops sell home surveillance equipment. Telephone bugs cost £20, and you can buy a chemical analysis kit on the Internet for £45 if you want proof, from the hair in your daughter's comb, for example, that she is taking drugs. Aerosol sprays and special chemical-soaked cotton wipes, as simple as home pregnancy kits, are available to see if there is cannabis or other narcotic residues on car seats or other surfaces.

Parental spies run the risk, if caught, of destroying the remnants of trust in their relationship with their children. But the trend is growing. Most American teenagers have telephones and televisions in their rooms, and many have computers and Internet access. Parents feel that they should be able to get to their children, even surreptitiously, because the rest of the world does.

The Daily Telegraph

??? COMPREHENSION

1 How are parents checking their children's behaviour?
2 What equipment is available to parents who want to spy on their children?
3 What risk is there, if the children find out?

ACTIVITIES

A Work together in groups of three or four. Imagine you have been asked for proposals from the government to reduce juvenile violence.
Think about:

- How children (boys and girls) could be better supervised
- How parents could be helped to monitor children's behaviour
- Policy on corporal punishment
- The age of criminal responsibility
- Whether there should be a group to represent youngsters' views

Discuss your ideas in groups, and come to a joint decision. Be prepared to justify your ideas. If you have more than one group on your class, compare your findings together and vote for the final proposals.

B Write an essay: I believe it is the parents' responsibility to teach children the difference between right and wrong.

DISCUSSION

1 At what age do you think children should be held responsible for their actions?

2 Is lack of parental supervision the main reason for the growth in female violence? If not, why not?

3 Are there any other causes responsible, such as female role models on television or computer game characters?

4 If you were a concerned parent, would you ever spy on your child – or do you think it is important to respect his/her privacy?

"We didn't have telly in wartime we had to make our own violence!"

5 Do you think that girls should be punished in the same way as boys – locked up in young offenders' institutes?

6 How do you think society can educate girls into being less violent?

7 Are girls becoming more violent in your own experience?

NETWORKING

Find out about teenage violence in your country. Are there TV programmes and films that promote juvenile violence?

Book: *Teenagers: the Agony, the Ecstasy, the Answers* by Aidan MacFarlane and Ann McPherson

Films: *Thelma and Louise* (1991) directed by Ridley Scott
Boyz 'n' the Hood (1991) directed by John Singleton

Websites:
www.nspcc.org.uk/
www.nbc.org.uk/

- What makes a good film? The plot, the actors, the special effects?
- Do you see many films that aren't made in Hollywood? If so, where are they from?

No sex, no violence, just film

Despite its severe Islamic censorship and taboos, Iranian cinema attracts a world cult following, says

Geoff Brown

Imagine yourself as a filmmaker in post-revolutionary Iran. Instead of shooting at Universal Studios, the venue for your creative labours is called The Studio of the Voice and Portrait of the Islamic Revolution of Iran.

Perhaps your cameras are out on location in the streets. Your film project has already jumped three censorship hurdles imposed by government agencies: synopsis approval, script approval, and cast and crew approval.

Now all that is left is to make the film, get the Government's final thumbs up, and be given an exhibition licence. But you cannot relax for one moment.

Your leading lady, should you have one, must not be a seductive beauty. Nor must there be any physical contact between male and female, even if the characters are man and wife or brother and sister. No violence, naturally. Nor can any character burst into song.

To the West, it may seem almost inconceivable that great and entertaining films could emerge from such restrictions, all put in place at different times since Iran's Islamic revolution. Yet each year a miracle happens. Iran's films are regularly invited to festivals, win prizes, including the Palme d'Or at

Cannes, and have become a cult among cinema aficionados.

To understand this remarkable phenomenon we must backtrack to the heights of the Islamic revolution in 1978-1979. 180 cinemas around the country were burnt down during the revolution – testament to the way films had come to be seen as part of the deposed Shah's Western leanings. Filmmakers set out into the new era timidly, afraid of treading on toes and risking punishment. Sticky areas such as religion were best

avoided altogether. Women, too, were for a time thought too hot to handle. But children seemed safe, and cheap, too.

Yet there was much more than expediency involved. Making films about youngsters' growing pains was an ideal way to do your bit for a society rebuilding itself around Muslim values.

Visually, such films tend to be as decorous and simple as their characters, far removed from Hollywood's bedlam. And the West loves them for it. When Iranian films first broke through internationally in the late Sixties, they seemed just one brand of exotica among many. Now they appear unique – films on a human scale, they refresh our jaded eyes.

Not that all Iranian cinema is classy enough to reach the West's cinema festivals and art houses. They make their dross, like everyone else. And a chasm sometimes exists between films aimed at local audiences and those obviously prepared to charm outsiders.

The best have the potential to please both camps, such as *The Apple* about two teenage daughters kept virtual prisoners by their father.

And paranoia can still rise up among government bodies. One part of the episode film, *Tales of Kish*, was withdrawn from the Fajr Film Festival, Iran's international showcase, because the 13-year-old heroine showed too much hair under her scarf.

Despite hints at thawing attitudes, an Iranian film that supinely apes Western ways is nowhere in sight. For all the chafing at individual restrictions, that must be a sign of artistic health.

The Times

COMPREHENSION

1 Where do Iranian film makers make their films?
2 How are Iranian leading ladies different from those in Hollywood?
3 Are Iranian films popular abroad? Justify your answer.
4 What are the advantages of using children in films?
5 Explain briefly in your own words how Iranian films are different.
6 How close are Iranian films to copying Western ones?

DISCUSSION

1 What are the strengths of Iranian films compared to ones from Hollywood?

2 What kind of films is Hollywood good at making?

3 What kind of films are made in your own country? Are they successful? Why, why not?

4 Do you prefer films produced in your country, or in Hollywood? Why?

5 Do you think Hollywood has too much power? If so, how can that be changed?

6 How have films changed over the last 20 years? Why do you think that is?

7 Do you think the cinema will still exist in 100 years' time? How will it have changed?

8 Will other countries ever be able to match the power of Hollywood to make films?

WE'VE DONE VOLCANO AND TWISTER. WE NEED ANOTHER MOVIE ABOUT A NATURAL DISASTER AND MY FIRST MARRIAGE CAME TO MIND.

ACTIVITIES

A Role-play: Work in groups of three or four. You are producers searching for a new blockbuster. Decide what kind of film you want to make – romance, thriller, science fiction.

Now decide how you will divide up your budget using the chart on the right. You have $100 million to spend and you have various options. Three stars is the highest quality – but the highest price! You can't have everything, so prioritise! Think carefully what type of film you are making, and that should help decide your budget.

Good luck!

	***	**	*
Star	$25 million	$15 million	$5 million
Supporting actors	$55 million	$35 million	$15 million
Director	$10 million	$5 million	$1 million
Locations/sets	$35 million	$22 million	$12 million
Costumes	$12 million	$8 million	$5 million
Script	$4 million	$2 million	$1 million
Music	$13 million	$8 million	$4 million
Special effects	$40 million	$17 million	$8 million

Compare your ideas with those of other groups – which group do you think has the best chance of having a hit?

B ✍ Write a review of the last film you saw that wasn't a Hollywood production. Give brief details of the plot, the film's strengths and weaknesses, and your recommendation. Read the reviews done by other students and, if you can, go and see the films.

NETWORKING

Find out about the film industry in your country. Compare styles of films made in different countries.

Books: *Easy Riders, Raging Bulls* by Peter Biskind
Halliwells' Film and Video Guide 2000 by John Walker
The Complete Film Dictionary by Ira Konigsburg

Films: *Boogie Nights* (1997) directed by Paul Thomas Anderson

Websites:
afi.cinemedia.org/

AMMUNITION BOX

Key words
production *the process of making a film*
to direct *to manage or control a film*
storyline *the events in the film*
performance *to act in a film or play*
score *the music that accompanies the film*
photography *the images of the film*

Handy hints
- Hollywood studios spend an average budget of $60 million on a film. However, they only make a profit a third of the time
- 'A' list stars of the late 20th century, such as Arnold Schwarzenegger and John Travolta, can earn over $20 million per film
- Indian cinema, known as 'Bollywood' is the world's largest producer of films with over 27,000 produced to date
- Americans, on average, go to the movies 4.5 times a year; Canadians, 2.8 times
- Video receipts bring in three times the amounts of film receipts

Key

v – verb	sb – somebody
n – noun	st – something
adj – adjective	coll – colloquial
adv – adverb	(am.) – American English
prep – preposition	

A

abdication /æbdɪˈkeɪʃn/ [8] *n* refusing to accept responsibility for st

absorb /əbzɔːb/ [52] *v* to become part of

abusive /əˈbjuːsɪv/ [40] *adj* rude

access /ˈækses/ [40] *v* to find information, especially on a computer

accessory /əkˈsesərɪ/ [18] *n* an item added to an oufit, a bag or necklace for example

accountable /əˈkaʊntəbl/ [44] *adj* responsible

accurate /ˈækjərət/ [52] *adj* exact, correct

acrobat /ˈækrəbæt/ [30] *n* a person who can do difficult or unusual physical actions

addicted /əˈdɪktɪd/ [40] *adj* liking st so much it is hard to stop

adjourn to /əˈdʒɜːn/ [6] *v* to go to another place

agnostic /ægˈnɒstɪk/ [38] *adj* a person who believes that people cannot know if God exists or not

alert /əˈlɜːt/ [12] *v* to let sb know

allege /əˈledʒ/ [8] *v* to say st is true without proof

amateurish /ˈæmətərɪʃ/ [26] *adj* not professional

amiable /ˈeɪmɪəbl/ [42] *adj* likeable

analysis /əˈnæləsɪs/ [58] *n* a detailed examination

anathema /əˈnæθəmə/ [6] *n* the opposite of what you believe in

animated /ˈænɪmeɪtɪd/ [6] *adj* lively

anxiety /æŋˈzaɪətɪ/ [36] *n* worry

arise /əˈraɪz/ [54] *v* to happen

assault /əˈsɔːlt/ [30] *n* an attack

assessment /əˈsesmənt/ [12] *n* a judgement

assume /əˈsjuːm/ [26] *v* to accept st is true before there is proof

astrology /əˈstrɒlədʒɪ/ [46] *n* the study of the stars and their influence on people

astronaut /ˈæˈstrənɔːt/ [38] *n* sb who travels to space

asylum /əˈsaɪləm/ [44] *n* political protection

awareness /əˈweənes/ [6] *n* knowledge of a particular situation

awesome /ˈɔːsəm/ [38] *adj* very impressive

B

backpack /ˈbækpæk/ [52] *v* to travel carrying your belongings on your back

ban /bæn/ [40] *n* when st is forbidden

bandwagon (jump on the) /ˈbændwægən/ [50] *n* to do st that other people are doing

banned /bænd/ [8] *adj* forbidden

barbaric /bɑːˈbærɪk/ [30] *adj* cruel

barracks /ˈbærəks/ [18] *n* the place where soldiers live

barrier /ˈbærɪə/ [6] *n* an object that prevents people from doing st

beacon /ˈbiːkən/ [42] *n* light

begrudge /bɪˈgrʌdʒ/ [32] *v* to resent

bend over backwards /ˈbend əʊvə ˈbækwədz/ [50] *v* to do everything you can

benefit /ˈbenɪfɪt/ [28] *n* advantage

benign /bɪˈnaɪn/ [42] *adj* gentle

beret /ˈbereɪ/ [18] *n* a round cap with a tight band around the head

bet /bet/ [42] *n* an arrangement that risks money

biased /ˈbaɪəst/ [44] *adj* strongly favouring one side in an argument

bidder /ˈbɪdə/ [2] *n* sb who offers a price in order to buy something

billed as /ˈbɪld æz/ [8] *adj* announced

blare /bleə/ [2] *v* to make a loud noise

bleak /bliːk/ [42] *adj* miserable

bleeding heart /bliːdɪŋ ˈhɑːt/ [50] *n* sb who is sympathetic to others

bloated /ˈbləʊtɪd/ [6] *adj* full of gas or liquid

blotter /ˈblɒtə/ [14] (am.) *n* a book where an official daily record is kept

boast /bəʊst/ [12] *v* to talk too proudly about your achievements

boundary /ˈbaʊndrɪ/ [12] *n* limit

bow /baʊ/ [14] *v* to give in to st

brace for /ˈbreɪs fɔː/ [50] *v* to prepare

bring sb up short /brɪŋ sʌmwʌn ʌp ʃɔːt/ [42] *v* to surprise sb

brood /bruːd/ [50] *n* children

bubble /ˈbʌbl/ [26] *n* a safe place

buckle up /bʌkl ˈʌp/ [14] *v* to put on seatbelts

bug /bʌg/ [58] *n* a small piece of equipment that listens to what people are saying

bumper to bumper /ˈbʌmpə tə bʌmpə/ [14] *adj* very heavy traffic

bustle /ˈbʌsl/ [34] *n* busy, noisy activity

buzz /bʌz/ [38] *adj* excitement

C

campaign /kæmˈpeɪn/ [30] *n* a series of actions to achieve a particular result

candidate /ˈkændɪdeɪt/ [38] *n* sb who is being considered for a job

carefree /ˈkeəfriː/ [38] *adj* having no worries

cast an eye over /ˈkɑːst ən ˈaɪ əʊvə/ [42] *v* to check st

cater for /ˈkeɪtə fɔː/ [52] *v* to provide people with what they need

Caucasian /kɔːˈkeɪʒn/ [48] *n* sb who is white or has pale skin

cease /siːs/ [30] *v* to stop

ceremony /ˈserəmənɪ/ [34] *n* a formal set of actions used at an important social or religious event

cheat /tʃiːt/ [8] *v* to behave in a dishonest way in order to gain an advantage

cheer /tʃɪə/ [16] *v* to celebrate

chew /tʃuː/ [22] *v* to bite on food

childless /ˈtʃaɪldləs/ [54] *adj* having no children

choke /tʃəʊk/ [2] *v* to prevent sb from breathing

chore /tʃɔː/ [34] *n* a job done to keep your house clean

cite /saɪt/ [16] *v* to mention

civilian /səˈvɪlɪən/ [18] *n* sb who is not a member of the army, navy, air force or police

cleric /ˈklerɪk/ [20] *n* a member of the clergy

cocoon /kəˈkuːn/ [26] *n* a protected area

collision /kəˈlɪʒn/ [14] *n* when two or more cars hit one another

colonialism /kəˈləʊnɪəlɪzm/ [30] *n* when a powerful country rules a weaker one

comb through /kəʊm ˈθruː/ [26] *v* to read very closely

compassion /kəmˈpæʃn/ [20] *adj* sympathy

compensation /kɒmpenˈseɪʃn/ [44] *n* money that sb pays you because they harmed you

compete /kəmˈpiːt/ [38] *v* to take part in a competition

compile /kəmˈpaɪl/ [42] *v* to make a list

complacency /kəmˈpleɪsənsɪ/ [50] *n* a feeling of self-satisfaction

complicated /ˈkɒmplɪkeɪtɪd/ [30] *adj* difficult to understand

comprise /kəmˈpraɪz/ [18] *v* to consist of particular parts

compulsion /kəmˈpʌlʃn/ [30] *n* a strong desire

compulsory /kəmˈpʌlsərɪ/ [22] *adj* st that has to be done

conceptual /kənˈseptʃuəl/ [6] *adj* based on underlying ideas

condemn /kən'dem/ [6] v to disapprove

condiment /'kɒndɪmənt/ [22] n st that you add to food to give it taste

condone /kən'dəʊn/ [8] v to forgive behaviour others think is odd

confinement /kən'faɪnmənt/ [42] n keeping sb in a place they cannot leave

confirm /kən'fɜ:m/ [4] v to say st is true

conflict /'kɒnflɪkt/ [20] n a state of disagreement

congested /kən'dʒestɪd/ [14] adj busy

conscientiously /kɒnʃɪ'enʃəslɪ/ [22] adv showing care and attention

consequence /'kɒnsɪkwens/ [38] n the results of an action

conspiracy /kən'spɪrəsɪ/ [8] n a secret plan

contrast /'kɒntra:st/ [42] n a difference

controversy /kən'trɒvəsɪ/ [54] n a disagreement

conversely /kən'vɜ:slɪ/ [8] adv in the opposite way

cornerstone /'kɔ:nəstəʊn/ [14] n st that is extremely important

cosmonaut /'kɒzmənɔ:t/ [38] n sb who travels to space (Russian)

couch potato /'kaʊtʃ pəteɪtəʊ/ [42] n sb who is very lazy

cramped /kræmpt/ [50] adj crowded

crater-pocked /'kreɪtəpɒkt/ [38] adj marked with holes

criminal /'krɪmɪnəl/ [50] adj awful

crony /'krəʊnɪ/ [34] n one of a group of people who know each other well

culprit /'kʌlprɪt/ [52] n sb who is guilty of a crime

curfew /'kɜ:fju:/ [34] n the time after which everyone must stay indoors

cyberspace /'saɪbəspeɪs/ [40] n the place where e-mails and information exist

D

dawn on /dɔ:n ɒn/ [28] v to realise

dazed /deɪzd/ [40] adj confused

decisive /dɪ'saɪsɪv/ [30] adj an action that has a powerful effect on a result

decorum /dɪ'kɔ:rʌm/ [26] n socially acceptable behaviour

decriminalise /di:'krɪmɪnəlaɪz/ [16] v to make st legal

defiant /dɪ'faɪənt/ [20] adj refusing to do what sb tells you

degraded /dɪ'greɪdɪd/ [42] adj humiliated

democratic /demə'krætɪk/ [24] adj controlled by people who are elected by the populace

depict /dɪ'pɪkt/ [42] v to represent

descendant /dɪ'sendənt/ [30] n related to sb who lived a long time ago

despise /dɪ'spaɪz/ [30] v to dislike sb

detract from /dɪ'trækt frɒm/ [28] v to reduce st

devoted to /dɪ'vəʊtɪd tu:/ [42] adj showing love and loyalty to sb

dialect /'daɪəlekt/ [30] n a language spoken only in one area

discipline /'dɪsəplɪn/ [12] n when people obey rules and orders

disguise /dɪs'gaɪz/ [46] v to hide st/sb so that people will not notice

disorientation /dɪs'ɔ:rɪənteɪʃn/ [30] n to be uncertain about what is happening

disregard /dɪsrɪ'gɑ:d/ [44] n ignoring st other people think is important

distinctive /dɪs'tɪŋktɪv/ [18] adj noticeable

distraught /dɪs'trɔ:t/ [44] adj very unhappy

diverse /daɪvɜ:s/ [24] adj different

doctrine /'dɒktrɪn/ [20] n belief

dominate /'dɒmɪneɪt/ [42] v to have power over st

donate /dəʊ'neɪt/ [34] v to give

donor /'dəʊnə/ [56] n sb that gives money

doodler /'du:dlə/ [48] n sb who draws shapes and patterns

dope /dəʊp/ [58] n drugs

download /daʊn'ləʊd/ [40] v to move information from one computer system to another

drag up /'dræg ʌp/ [50] v to bring up children

drained of /'dreɪnd əv/ [36] adj lacking energy

draining /'dreɪnɪŋ/ [40] adj tiring

drill sergeant /'drɪl sɑ:dʒənt/ [38] n so in the army who shouts out orders

drop out /drɒp 'aʊt/ [50] v to leave school or college early

dungheap /'dʌŋhi:p/ [42] n a pile of waste from animals

duped /'dju:pt/ [6] adj deceived

E

eager /'i:gə/ [2] adj enthusiastic

echo /'ekəʊ/ [44] n a repeat of a sound

ego /'i:gəʊ/ [38] n the opinion you have about yourself

element /'elɪmənt/ [30] n part

eligible /'elɪdʒəbl/ [12] adj suitable

embrace /ɪm'breɪs/ [20] n a hug

embryo /'embrɪəʊ/ [54] n the very early stages of development in the womb

emerge /ɪ'mɜ:dʒ/ [40] v to appear

emit /ɪ'mɪt/ [2] v to produce

encircle /en'sɜ:kl/ [12] v to surround

encrusted /ɪn'krʌstɪd/ [18] adj covered with

endangered /ɪn'deɪndʒəd/ [24] adj in danger

endurance /ɪn'djʊərəns/ [50] n the ability to suffer patiently

endure /ɪn'djʊə/ [30] v to suffer patiently

enforced /ɪn'fɔ:st/ [20] adj forced

enforcement /ɪn'fɔ:smənt/ [14] n making sure a law is effective

engage in /ɪn'geɪdʒ ɪn/ [14] v to become involved in

enigmatically /enɪg'mætɪklɪ/ [6] adv mysteriously

epidemic /epɪ'demɪk/ [20] n the rapid spread of a disease

equate /ɪ'kweɪt/ [20] v to consider st equal

eradicate /ɪ'rædɪkeɪt/ [30] v to wipe out

erupt /ɪ'rʌpt/ [14] v to breakout

estimated /'estɪmeɪtɪd/ [12] adj roughly calculated

ethical /'eθɪkəl/ [44] adj relating to moral principles

ethnic /'eθnɪk/ [44] adj a race or tribe with a common cultural tradition

evolution /i:və'lu:ʃn/ [42] n the gradual development of characteristics over many years

exemplary /ɪg'zemplərɪ/ [36] adj a good example

exiled /'eksaɪld/ [52] adj living away from your country

expand /ɪk'spænd/ [24] v to increase in size

expression /ɪk'spreʃən/ [30] n the action of making your feelings known

exquisite /ɪk'sgwɪzɪt/ [18] adj beautiful

extend /ɪk'stend/ [24] v to make something longer

extracted /ɪk'stræktɪd/ [54] adj taken from

extreme /ɪk'stri:m/ [14] adj very great

F

fade away /feɪd ə'weɪ/ [30] v to die out

failsafe /'feɪlseɪf/ [52] adj st that always works

fan /fæn/ [12] n a person who admires sb/st very strongly

fat-cat /fæt'kæt/ [42] n a person who is rich and powerful

feature /'fi:tʃə/ [44] v to appear in a newspaper or magazine

fed up /fed 'ʌp/ [28] adj unhappy

fight tooth and nail /faɪt 'tu:θ ænd 'neɪl/ [12] v to fight with all your might

file /faɪl/ [44] v to send in a news story

final /'faɪnl/ [30] adj last

finger-pointing /'fɪŋgəpɔɪntɪŋ/ [50] adj accusing

first-time buyer /fɜ:staɪm 'baɪə/ [28] n sb who buys property for the first time

flattering /'flætərɪŋ/ [44] adj praising

fleece /fli:s/ [50] v to take money from sb

flounder /'flaʊndə/ [22] n a small, flatfish

fortuitously /fɔ:'tʃu:ɪtəslɪ/ [38] adv luckily

foster /'fɒstə/ [56] v to help the development of sb

foundation /faʊn'deɪʃn/ [18] n make up

fragile /'frædʒaɪl/ [4] adj easily damaged

frantic /'fræntɪk/ [8] adj in a state of great anxiety

funding /'fʌndɪŋ/ [8] n supporting financially

G

gallumphing /gə'lʌmfɪŋ/ [52] *adj* walking heavily

gear /gɪə/ [18] *n* clothes

gene /dʒiːn/ [54] *n* a unit in a chromosome which controls inherited characteristics

generate /'dʒenəreɪt/ [44] *v* to produce st

germ /dʒɜːm/ [56] *n* an organism that causes disease

gesture /'dʒestʃə/ [8] *n* an action

get one's knickers in a twist /'get wʌnz 'nɪkəz ɪn ə 'twɪst/ [50] *v* to get into a state of anxiety

ghetto /'getəʊ/ [52] *n* an area lived in by a particular type of person

gibbering /'dʒɪbərɪŋ/ [30] *n* speaking in a confused way

gigantic /dʒaɪ'gæntɪk/ [24] *adj* very big

global warming /'gləʊbl'wɔːmɪŋ/ [14] *n* an increase in temperature of the earth's atmosphere

grab /græb/ [32] *v* to take st quickly

grant /grɑːnt/ [6] *v* to give st formally to sb

grassroots /grɑː'sruːts/ [24] *n* ordinary people in society

gravity /'grævɪtɪ/ [36] *n* importance

grief /griːf/ [30] *n* unhappiness

grotesque /grəʊ'tesk/ [42] *adj* ugly

H

handicapped /'hændɪkæpt/ [55] *adj* disabled

hang out with /hæŋ'aʊtwɪð/ [52] *v* to spend time with people

harassment /hə'ræsmənt/ [44] *n* bothering sb

hard luck case /haːd 'lʌkeɪs/ [50] *n* a sad story

harvested /'haːvɪstɪd/ [54] *adj* collected

hashish /hæ'fiːʃ/ [16] *n* marijuana

hazardous /'hæzədəs/ [14] *adj* dangerous

head off /hed'ɒf/ [36] *v* to avoid

heiress /eə'res/ [18] *n* a woman who will inherit a lot of money

henpecked /'henpekt/ [34] *adj* a bullied husband

heritage /'herətɪdʒ/ [30] *n* customs that have been continued from earlier generations

high /haɪ/ [16] *n* a feeling of great happiness

hinder /'hɪndə/ [20] *v* to delay

hippy /'hɪpɪ/ [59] *adj* a rejection of organised society and social habits, begun in the 1960s

hit /hɪt/ [46] *n* do st successfully

holier than thou /'həʊlɪə ðən 'ðaʊ/ [50]
adj thinking yourself morally superior

homosexuality /'həʊmə'sekʃʊælətɪ/ [20] *n* being sexually attracted to sb of the same sex as yourself

hooligan /'huːlɪgən/ [42] *n* a young person who is violent and noisy (usually male)

horde /hɔːd/ [36] *n* a large crowd of people

hormone /'hɔːməʊn/ [54] *n* a substance produced within the body

horrified /'hɒrɪfaɪd/ [18] *adj* shocked

hunched /hʌntʃt/ [34] *adj* crouched

hunter-gatherer /'hʌntə'gæðərə/ [30] *n* sb who looked for food (animals and berries) when man was still a cave dweller

hurricane /'hʌrɪkən/ [46] *n* a violent storm with strong winds

hybrid /'haɪbrɪd/ [56] *n* an animal or plant with parents of different species

I

identify with /aɪ'dentɪfaɪ/ [48] *v* to regard sb/st as sharing the same characteristics as yourself

immoral /ɪ'mɒrəl/ [18] *adj* morally wrong

immune system /ɪ'mjuːn'sɪstəm/ [56] *n* the system that helps the body fight disease

immune to /ɪ'mjuːntuː/ [36] *adj* not affected or influenced by st

impact /'ɪmpækt/ [22] *n* a strong impression or effect

impediment /ɪm'pedɪmənt/ [24] *n* st that delays or stops progress

implanted /ɪm'plɑːntɪd/ [54] *adj* tissue inserted into a part of the body

impose /ɪm'pəʊz/ [2] *v* to force certain ·beliefs or cultures onto sb

imposing /ɪm'pəʊzɪŋ/ [24] *adj* impressive

imprudent /ɪm'pruːdənt/ [34] *adj* unwise

indigenous /ɪn'dɪʒənəs/ [30] *adj* native

indignant /ɪn'dɪgnənt/ [28] *adj* cross

indulgence /ɪn'dʌlgəns/ [6] *n* being allowed to do whatever you want

infertile /ɪn'fɜːtaɪl/ [54] *adj* unable to reproduce

infrastructure /'ɪnfrəstrʌktʃə/ [14] *n* basic structures and facilities

ingest /ɪn'dʒest/ [18] *v* to eat

initiate /ɪ'nɪʃɪeɪt/ [14] *v* to start

insist on /ɪn'sɪst ɒn/ [28] *v* to demand st forcefully

insomnia /ɪn'sɒmnɪə/ [20] *n* being unable to sleep

install /ɪn'stɔːl/ [12] *v* to fit

insult /ɪn'sʌlt/ [34] *v* to speak in a way that offends sb

irrecoverable /ɪrɪ'kʌvərəbl/ [30] *adj* lost

irregularity /ɪ'regjəlærətɪ/ [44] *n*
contrary to what is established

irrespective of /ɪrɪ'spektɪv əv/ [20] *prep* not taking st into account

irreversibly /ɪrɪ'vɜːsɪblɪ/ [52] *adv* st that cannot be changed back

J

juvenile /'dʒuːvənaɪl/ [46] *adj* young

K

keen /kiːn/ [12] *adj* enthusiastic

khaki /'kɑːkɪ/ [18] *n* a dark green colour used for military uniforms

kitsch /kɪtʃ/ [10] *adj* cheap, showy

knock out /'nɒk aʊt/ [16] *v* to make you sleepy

L

lager lout /'lɑːgə laʊt/ [42] *n* sb who behaves badly while drunk (usually male)

larger-than-life /'lɑːdʒə ðæn 'laɪf/ [42] *adj* very realistic

laxity /'læksətɪ/ [8] *n* not strict

leak /liːk/ [54] *n* revealed information

legalise /'liːgəlaɪz/ [16] *v* to make st legal

legitimate /lɪ'dʒɪtəmət/ [16] *adj* lawful

lewd /ljuːd/ [40] *adj* rude

licence /'laɪsns/ [22] *n* allowing sb to do st

limousine /lɪmə'ziːn/ [26] *n* a large luxurious car

livelihood /'laɪvlɪhʊd/ [24] *n* a means of living

lobby /'lɒbɪ/ [14] *v* to try to persuade the government that st should change

logical /'lɒdʒɪkl/ [36] *adj* sensible

loophole /'luːphəʊl/ [46] *n* a way of avoiding st

ludicrous /'luːdɪkrəs/ [46] *adj* absurd

M

mall /mæl/ [36] *n* a large shopping centre (am.)

man /mæn/ [38] *v* to operate st with men or women

marginal /'mɑːdʒɪnəl/ [30] *adj* having little importance

mass /mæs/ [22] *n* a large quantity

mass-produced /mæs prə'djuːst/ [2] *adj* when large quantities are manufactured

mate /meɪt/ [28] *n* friend

mean-spirited /miːn'spɪrɪtɪd/ [32] *adj* ungenerous

medium /'miːdɪəm/ [48] *n* a means by which st is expressed or communicated

mindless /'maɪndləs/ [2] *adj* serving no useful purpose

miscarriage /'mɪskærɪdʒ/ [54] *n* giving birth to a baby that doesn't survive in the early stages of pregnancy

miscarriage of justice /ˈmɪskærɪdʒ əv ˈdjʌstɪs/ [44] *n* when sb is found guilty of a crime of which they are innocent

mishap /ˈmɪshæp/ [12] *n* a small accident

mislead /mɪsˈliːd/ [6] *v* to give sb the wrong idea

misrepresentation /mɪsreprɪzenˈteɪtʃən/ [44] *n* when st is represented wrongly

mission /ˈmɪʃn/ [38] *n* a task

mix-up /ˈmɪksʌp/ [54] *n* a confused situation

monitor /ˈmɒnɪtə/ [8] *v* to check

moral /ˈmɒrəl/ [8] *adj* concerned with principles of right or wrong

morality /məˈrælətɪ/ [8] *n* principles concerned with right or wrong

mortal /ˈmɔːtəl/ [50] *n* a human being

mortgage /ˈmɔːgɪdʒ/ [28] *n* money lent by a bank to buy property

mount an exhibition /maunt æn eksɪˈbɪtʃn/ [6] *v* to put on an exhibition

N

nag /næg/ [38] *v* to complain continuously

new-age /njuːˈeɪdʒ/ [46] *adj* rejecting modern values

newsworthy /ˈnjuːzwɜːði/ [44] *adj* interesting

norm /nɔːm/ [14] *n* standard

notorious /nəʊˈtɔːrɪəs/ [28] *adj* infamous

O

obese /əʊˈbiːs/ [4] *adj* very fat

obligation /ɒblɪˈgeɪtʃn/ [28] *n* promise

obtuse /əbˈtjuːs/ [40] *adj* difficult

offspring /ˈɒfsprɪŋ/ [54] *n* children

oppressor /əˈpresə/ [30] *n* sb who treats people harshly

optimism /ˈɒptɪmɪzm/ [42] *n* expecting the best in all things

optimistic /ɒptɪˈmɪstɪk/ [46] *adj* confident

ordeal /ɔːˈdɪəl/ [26] *n* a difficult event

organic /ɔːˈgænɪk/ [22] *adj* when food is produced without artificial chemicals

outbreak /ˈaʊtbreɪk/ [20] *n* the sudden appearance of a disease

outdated /aʊtˈdeɪtɪd/ [10] *adj* old-fashioned

outlandish /aʊtˈlændɪʃ/ [26] *adj* strange

outlaw /ˈaʊtlɔː/ [14] *v* to ban

output /ˈaʊtpʊt/ [2] *n* the amount that an organisation or person produces

outrage /ˈaʊtreɪdʒ/ [44] *n* a strong feeling of anger and shock

outrageous /aʊtˈreɪdʒəs/ [6] *adj* shocking

ovaries /ˈəʊvəriz/ [54] *n* the organs in females that produce eggs

overbearing /əʊvəˈbeərɪŋ/ [28] *adj* dominating

overturn /əʊvəˈtɜːn/ [8] *v* to reverse a decision

P

package /ˈpækɪdʒ/ [52] *n* a holiday organised by a travel agent

packed with /ˈpækt wɪð/ [52] *adj* full of

pamper /ˈpæmpə/ [50] *v* to treat sb with too much kindness

panic /ˈpænɪk/ [34] *n* feeling of great fear

parishioner /pəˈrɪʃənə/ [20] *n* sb who goes to church regularly

partisan /ˈpɑːtɪzæn/ [26] *adj* enthusiastic, uncritical

patented /ˈpeɪtəntɪd/ [24] *adj* when an object can only be produced or sold by one person and no one can make a copy

patriotism /ˈpætrɪətɪzm/ [42] *n* love of your country

peddler /ˈpedlə/ [2] *n* sb who promotes certain ideas

peer /pɪə/ [34] *v* to look closely at st

pejorative /pəˈdʒɒrətɪv/ [2] *adj* expressing contempt or disapproval

penalise /ˈpiːnəlaɪz/ [24] *v* to punish sb for breaking the law

penetrate /ˈpenɪtreɪt/ [2] *v* to make a way into st

perception /pɜːˈseptʃn/ [4] *n* understanding st

perennial /pəˈrenɪəl/ [4] *adj* constantly occurring

persistent /pɜːˈsɪstənt/ [30] *adj* refusing to give up

pervert /ˈpɜːvɜːt/ [40] *n* sb whose behaviour (esp. sexual) is considered odd

pervy /ˈpɜːvɪ/ [40] *adj* odd (esp. sexual) behaviour

pessimistic /pesɪˈmɪstɪk/ [46] *adj* always expecting the worst

pet interest /pet ˈɪntərest/ [48] *n* a main interest

pettiness /ˈpetɪnes/ [32] *n* unimportant things

pipe out /paɪp ˈaʊt/ [40] *v* to play out music

plaudit /ˈplɔːdɪt/ [48] *n* praise

plight /plaɪt/ [44] *n* a difficult situation

politically correct /pəˈlɪtɪklɪ kəˈrekt/ [10] *adj* taking care not to offend people

poll /pəʊl/ [46] *n* a vote

portray /pɔːˈtreɪ/ [48] *v* to present

potent /ˈpəʊtənt/ [44] *adj* powerful

pound /paʊnd/ [36] *v* to knock loudly

preach /priːtʃ/ [20] *v* to make a religious speech

predict /prɪdɪkt/ [54] *v* to say in advance that st will happen

predictability /prɪˈdɪktəˈbɪlɪtɪ/ [52] *n* st that is unsurprising

prediction /prɪˈdɪktʃn/ [46] *n* st that is forecast

prejudice /ˈpredjuːdɪs/ [20] *n* dislike of a certain group of people

prevalence /ˈprevələns/ [20] *n* st that is widespread

prise open /praɪz ˈəʊpən/ [24] *v* to force st open

producitivity /prɒdʌkˈtɪvətɪ/ [32] *n* producing goods

prominent /ˈprɒmɪnənt/ [42] *adj* easily seen

promote /prəˈməʊt/ [20] *v* to encourage

prompt /prɒmpt/ [22] *v* to cause a feeling of action

progressive /prəˈgresɪv/ [16] *adj* favouring reform

pros and cons /ˈprəʊz ənd ˈkɒnz/ [28] *n* the advantages and disadvantages

protectionist /prəˈtekʃnɪst/ [2] *adj* when a country protects its own industries

provision /prəˈvɪʃn/ [24] *n* the amount of st that is provided

punish /ˈpʌnɪʃ/ [8] *v* to make sb suffer for having broken the law

Q

quintuple /kwɪnˈtjuːpl/ [24] *v* to increase by four

R

raft /rɑːft/ [22] *n* a large number

rarity /ˈreərɪtɪ/ [34] *n* st that is unusual

rate /reɪt/ [50] *n* a measurement

ratify /ˈrætɪfaɪ/ [24] *v* to make a contract

ratio /ˈreɪʃɪəʊ/ [58] *n* a relation between two amounts

ration /ˈræʃn/ [4] *n* a fixed quantity of food

raucous /ˈrɔːkəs/ [34] *adj* noisy

reactionary /rɪˈækʃənrɪ/ [2] *adj* opposing reform

recipient /rɪˈsɪpɪənt/ [26] *n* sb who receives st

recline /rɪˈklaɪn/ [34] *v* to lie down

reflect /rɪˈflekt/ [48] *v* to think about st

regime /reɪˈʒiːm/ [4] *n* a method

rehabilitation /riːhəbɪlɪˈteɪtʃn/ [12] *n* when sb lives an active, useful life after prison

reinstatement /riːɪnˈsteɪtmənt/ [30] *n* when st is restored to its previous position

relaxation /riːlækˈseɪtʃn/ [8] *n* rest

relentless /rɪˈlentləs/ [42] *adj* never-ending

remnants /ˈremnənts/ [58] *n* the remains

renounce /rɪˈnaʊns/ [22] *n* to give up

rent /rent/ [28] *v* a regular payment for the use of st (a house)

repressive /rɪˈpresɪv/ [30] *adj* harsh

reschedule /riːˈʃedjuːl/ [36] *i* to change the time of st

residue /ˈrezɪdjuː/ [58] *n* remains

resist /rɪˈzɪst/ [4] *v* to oppose a plan

resort to /rɪˈzɔːt/ [58] *v* to make use of st as a final measure

retinue /ˈretɪnjuː/ [26] *n* a group of attendants

retreat /rɪˈtriːt/ [26] *n* a safe place

retrieve /rɪˈtriːv/ [58] *v* to find

revoked /rɪˈvəʊkt/ [12] *adj* taken away

righteousness /ˈraɪtʃəsnəs/ [8] *n* st that is morally justified

role-reversal /ˈrəʊlrɪvɜːəl/ [34] *n* to swap roles

rule the roost /ˈruːl ðə ˈruːst/ [34] *v* to be in charge

ruling /ˈruːlɪŋ/ [28] *n* an official decision

S

safeguard /ˈseɪfgɑːd/ [24] *v* to protect

salary /ˈsælərɪ/ [28] *n* money you are paid for work

sanction /ˈsæŋkʃn/ [24] *v* to give permission

sane /seɪn/ [40] *adj* mentally healthy

sangria /ˈsæŋgrɪə/ [6] *n* a Spanish drink made with red wine, lemonade and fruit

sanitise /ˈsænɪtaɪz/ [10] *v* to make st more acceptable

savour /ˈseɪvə/ [4] *v* to enjoy

scandal /ˈskændəl/ [46] *n* an event considered shocking

scepticism /ˈskeptɪsɪzm/ [46] *n* doubting that a claim is true

scheme /skiːm/ [12] *n* a plan

scrub /skrʌb/ [34] *v* to clean thoroughly

security /sɪkˈjʊərətɪ/ [16] *n* freedom from worry

seedy /ˈsiːdɪ/ [40] *adj* not respectable

seek /siːk/ [44] *v* to try

seek to /ˈsiːk tuː/ [30] *v* to try to

selective /sɪlektɪv/ [24] *adj* choosy

self-righteous /selfˈraɪtʃəs/ [14] *adj* acting as if you are always right

separatist /ˈseprətɪst/ [42] *n* sb who stays separate from other people

servile /ˈsɜːvaɪl/ [34] *adj* too willing to serve others

set /set/ [6] *adj* fixed

set at naught /ˈset ɑːt ˈnɔːt/ [24] *v* to ignore

shift /ʃɪft/ [20] *n* a change

shoot a film /ˈʃuːt ə ˈfɪlm/ [60] *v* to make a film

shortage /ˈʃɔːtɪdʒ/ [56] *n* a lack of

showdown /ˈʃəʊdaʊn/ [36] *n* climax

side-effect /ˈsaɪdɪfekt/ [4] *n* an unpleasant effect, usually of a drug

sizzling /ˈsɪzlɪŋ/ [22] *adj* hot

slammer /ˈslæmə/ [50] *n* prison (coll.)

slap down /slæp daʊn/ [24] *v* to refuse

slash /slæʃ/ [26] *v* to reduce

slim /slɪm/ [12] *adj* thin

slobbish /ˈslɒbɪʃ/ [42] *adj* lazy

slogan /ˈsləʊgən/ [24] *n* a word or phrase used by a political party

slot /slɒt/ [42] *n* a space

smart /smɑːt/ [18] *adj* well-dressed

smuggle /ˈsmʌgl/ [44] *v* to take illegal goods in or out of a country

snack /snæk/ [4] *n* a small meal

sniffer dog /ˈsnɪfə dɒg/ [58] *n* a dog that is trained to sniff out drugs

snort /snɔːt/ [28] *v* to laugh loudly

soothsayer /ˈsuːθseɪə/ [46] *n* sb who can predict the future

speculate /ˈspekjuleɪt/ [36] *v* to form opinions without having thought about them

spectre /ˈspektə/ [4] *n* a ghost

spew out /spjuːˈaʊt/ [42] *v* to vomit

splash out on /ˈsplæʃ aʊt ɒn/ [18] *v* to spend a lot of money on st

sponsor /ˈspɒnsə/ [60] *n* a person or firm who pays for st

sponsorship /ˈspɒnsəʃɪp/ [6] *n* the money given for a specified activity

sprint /sprɪnt/ [8] *v* to run a short distance very fast

spy /spaɪ/ [58] *v* to collect secret information

stability /stˈbɪlətɪ/ [16] *n* the state of being fixed

staple /ˈsteɪpl/ [22] *n* standard

startling /ˈstɑːtlɪŋ/ [22] *adj* surprising

stereotype /ˈsterɪətaɪp/ [42] *n* a fixed idea

stigma /ˈstɪgmə/ [50] *n* a bad reputation

stigmatised /ˈstɪgmətaɪzd/ [12] *adj* disapproved of

stride /straɪd/ [42] *v* to walk with long steps

striking /ˈstraɪkɪŋ/ [58] *adj* interesting

strip sb of st /strɪp ɒv/ [8] *v* to take st away from sb

struggle /ˈstrʌgl/ [4] *v* to fight against

studs /stʌdz/ [18] *n* small earrings

stunt /stʌnt/ [6] *n* st done to attract attention

subservient /səbˈsɜːvɪənt/ [34] *adj* to be too obedient

subsidy /ˈsʌbsədɪ/ [24] *n* money paid by the government to organisations

substance /ˈsʌbstəns/ [8] *n* drug

sue /suː/ [8] *v* to start a legal case against sb

sullenly /ˈsʌlənlɪ/ [4] *adj* in a bad tempered way

sum /sʌm/ [30] *n* total

superior /suːpɪərɪə/ [48] *adj* more important

supervision /suːpəˈvɪʃn/ [58] *n* checking what sb does

supportive /səˈpɔːtɪv/ [38] *adj* giving help

surreptitiously /sʌrəpˈtɪʃəslɪ/ [58] *adj* doing st discretely

surveillance /səˈveɪləns/ [58] *n* watching sb secretly

surveyor /səˈveɪə/ [28] *n* a person who examines buildings

survive /səˈvaɪv/ [40] *v* to continue to live

sustain /səˈsteɪn/ [30] *v* to keep sb/st alive

swap /swɒp/ [8] *v* to exchange

sway /sweɪ/ [26] *v* to change sb's opinion

swell /swel/ [38] *v* to grow bigger

swifty /ˈswɪftɪ/ [36] *n* a quick drink (coll.)

swig /swɪg/ [34] *n* a gulp of a drink

synopsis /sɪˈnɒpsɪs/ [60] *n* a summary

T

tab /tæb/ [6] *n* a bill of drinks kept behind the bar

taboo /təˈbuː/ [20] *adj* a cultural or religious custom that stops people talking about subjects

tackle /ˈtækl/ [12] *v* to talk about

tailgate /ˈteɪlgeɪt/ [14] *v* to drive very close to the person in front

tailor to /ˈteɪlə tuː/ [12] *v* to be specially made for sb

tamper-proof /ˈtæmpəpruːf/ [12] *adj* cannot be altered

testimony /ˈtestɪmənɪ/ [44] *n* a statement

tiara /tɪˈɑːrə/ [10] *n* a very small crown

tolerate /ˈtɒləreɪt/ [16] *v* to endure

to no avail /tuː nəʊ əˈveɪl/ [44] pointless

torrent /ˈtɒrənt/ [60] *n* a mass

torso /ˈtɔːsəʊ/ [60] *n* the main part of the human body minus head, arms and legs

tot /tɒt/ [54] *n* small child

toxic /ˈtɒksɪk/ [2] *adj* poisonous

toxin /ˈtɒksɪn/ [22] *n* poison

trace /treɪs/ [8] *n* the remains of a drug in the body

track down /trækˈdaʊn/ [58] *v* to look for sb

tracksuit /ˈtræksjuːt/ [18] *n* casual sportswear

trainers /ˈtreɪnəz/ [18] *n* soft shoes worn by sportspeople

transplant /trænˈzɪʃn/ [56] *v* to plant tissue or an organ from one person (or animal) to another person

treaty /ˈtriːtɪ/ [24] *n* a formal agreement between countries

trend /trend/ [58] *n* a tendency

tribe /traɪb/ [30] *n* a group of people of the same race

typical /ˈtɪpɪkl/ [20] *adj* characteristic

U

ubiquitous /juːˈbɪkwɪtəs/ [52] *adj* seeming to be everywhere

uncontroversial /ˌʌnkɒntrəˈvɜːʃl/ [24]

adj not likely to cause disagreement

uniform /ˈjuːnɪfɔːm/ [18] *n* the set of clothes worn by all members of an organisation

unleash /ʌnˈliːʃ/ [24] *v* to release

unmitigated /ʌnˈmɪtɪɡeɪtɪd/ [16] *adj* complete, absolute

unwieldy /ʌnˈwiːldɪ/ [42] *adj* difficult to move

unwitting /ʌnˈwɪtɪŋ/ [22] *adj* doing st without being aware of it

ups and downs /ʌps ənd ˈdaʊnz/ [40] *n* positive and negative things

urge /ɜːdʒ/ [20] *v* to encourage

usher /ˈʌʃə/ [6] *v* to escort

V

vague /veɪɡ/ [46] *adj* not definite

venture /ˈventʃə/ [24] *v* to go out

vilify /ˈvɪlɪfaɪ/ [26] *v* to insult

violation /vaɪəˈleɪʃn/ [8] *n* when the law is broken

virtually /ˈvɜːtʃuəlɪ/ [44] *adv* almost

virtuous /ˈvɜːtʃuəs/ [32] *adj* having high moral principles

virus /ˈvaɪrəs/ [20] *n* st that causes disease

vital /ˈvaɪtəl/ [28] *adj* essential

vividly /ˈvɪvɪdlɪ/ [38] *adv* clearly

volunteer /vɒlənˈtɪə/ [38] *n* sb who works without pay

vulnerable /ˈvʌnrəbl/ [20] *adj* that can be easily hurt

W

wallet /ˈwɒlɪt/ [18] *n* where money is kept

wardrobe /ˈwɔːdrəʊb/ [18] *n* sb's collection of clothes

weed /wiːd/ [16] *n* marijuana (coll.)

well-connected /welkəˈnektɪd/ [44] *adj* to be friendly with influential people

womb /wuːm/ [54] *n* the organ in which the baby is carried while it develops

worthier /wɜːðɪə/ [6] *adj* better

worthwhile /wɜːθˈwaɪl/ [38] *adj* important

Y

yield /jiːld/ [60] *v* to produce